OPEN SECRET

The Kissinger-Nixon Doctrine in Asia

OPEN SECRET

The Kissinger-Nixon Doctrine in Asia

Edited by

VIRGINIA BRODINE
and MARK SELDEN

INTRODUCTION BY NOAM CHOMSKY

PERENNIAL LIBRARY
Harper & Row, Publishers
New York · Evanston · San Francisco · London

OPEN SECRET: THE KISSINGER-NIXON DOCTRINE IN ASIA

A publication of the Foreign Policy Round Table with the cooperation of the Committee of Concerned Asian Scholars.

A portion of "Henry Kissinger's Diplomacy of Force" by Virginia Brodine and Mark Selden appeared in slightly different form in the January 30, 1972, issue of *The Nation*.

An expanded version of "The Geography of Empire" by Keith Buchanan appeared in the Spring 1972 issue of the *Bulletin of Concerned Asian Scholars*.

"Asia and the Nixon Doctrine: The New Face of Empire" by John Dower is a much expanded and revised version of an article that appeared originally in the Fall 1970 issue of the *Bulletin of Concerned Asian Scholars*.

Introduction copyright © by Noam Chomsky

First PERENNIAL LIBRARY edition published 1972

LIBRARY OF CONGRESS CATALOG CARD NUMBER: 72–82895

STANDARD BOOK NUMBER: 06–080253–7

CONTENTS

INTRODUCTION

NOAM CHOMSKY

The essays that follow present a searching—and I believe persuasive—analysis of the Nixon-Kissinger foreign policy, its roots in postwar American global strategy, and some of the likely consequences. If the questions raised here are neglected, as they have been in the recent past, the cost to us as well as to the victims of American power will be severe. Fortunately, conditions are favorable for such inquiry. Although the executive branch of the government continues to exercise its vast power behind a veil of secrecy and deceit, often in direct violation of congressional statute as well as valid treaties, nevertheless there is now sufficient skepticism and open-mindedness among the general public and segments of Congress so that the American role in world affairs can be broadly considered and debated. The suffocating ideological consensus of the postwar years has, at last, collapsed. It is generally recognized that the standard pieties offer a poor guide to the realities of international affairs, and in the current much more healthy intellectual climate, foreign policy can become a topic of serious discussion.

These essays interpret the Nixon-Kissinger policies

as an attempt to adapt imperial strategy to changing patterns of world power, taking account of certain constraints that even a superpower cannot blithely ignore. The authors trace the general outlines of the U.S.-Japan Pacific system as part of a global system of economic, military, and cultural domination. They proceed to disentangle and examine critically the major assumptions of the Nixon-Kissinger approach to "a world order based on U.S. supremacy" as it has evolved and is now being pursued. Their conclusions are grim, but, I think, realistic.

If the aims of American policy are granted, the Nixon-Kissinger approach may be rational, though it is far from riskless. There are competing interests that divide the industrial powers within the system. Furthermore, resistance will continue on the part of those who seek a different path to social and economic development, and who do not comprehend the transcendent importance of guaranteeing to the industrial powers a limitless flow of resources and unrestricted opportunities for investment. Nor can the threat of nuclear war be discounted, as the superpowers maneuver to repress the striving for independence within the systems they dominate and on the unsettled frontiers of empire. In fact, it has been plausibly argued that the Nixon-Kissinger approach to "security" lowers the nuclear threshold and thus increases the probability of a final disaster.

There is, however, no legitimate reason for the public to adopt as its own the objectives that guide American global policy. On the contrary, elementary decency demands a sympathetic concern for the efforts of the poor to overcome the awesome problems of social and economic development even if this leads them to take control of their own resources and extricate themselves from the imperial systems. Furthermore, the costs and risks of imperial domination are not slight, and, as in the past, they are borne by the population of the imperial societies as a whole.

As a general rule, an imperial power is guided by the "national interest" as conceived and defined by dominant social groups. At the same time, its ideologists labor to mask this pursuit of self-interest with a system of delusion and mystification. To be effective, this belief system must, of course, bear some relationship to reality, and often it will appear convincing not only to the mass of the population but to policy makers and ideologists as well—a matter of some significance. Use of the term "national interest" is one familiar technique of mystification. The ideologists of empire rarely ask who pays and who profits.

The administrators of subjugated societies often share and contribute to the delusional system. They persuade themselves that they are bringing enlightenment and modern, progressive institutional structures to the benighted masses, incapable of raising themselves from poverty and degradation by their own efforts. The colonial administrators are engaged in "nation building," as in Vietnam, where they must reconstruct a society shattered by bombs and napalm and integrate it into the Free World. Quite naturally, these "agents of modernization" cannot understand why they are regarded as war criminals, just as they are unaware of the levels of ignorance, stupidity, and arrogance revealed by the description of their activities as "nation building" in Vietnam.

The cold war has provided a convenient framework for the apologists of imperial domination, while at the same time threatening the imperial powers themselves with total disaster. Washington claims to be defending democracy and warding off "internal aggression" by agents of international communism when it destroys a mass popular movement in Greece, subverts the nationalist government of Iran, supports an invasion of Guatemala, invades the Dominican Republic and devastates the peasant societies of Indochina. Its defenders, and many critics as well, are at most willing to concede error if plans go awry, and cannot conceive that any "responsible" or "qualified" observer might have a rather different view. Similarly, when the Soviet Union deploys its armies to control its East European satellites, its spokesmen depict it as defending socialism and protecting the population from West German aggression or the machinations of the CIA and Wall Street. They too, no doubt, are bewildered at the bitter response to Russian sacrifice and benevolence.

It must be emphasized again that, like the delusional systems that individuals may construct in their personal lives, the propaganda images of the superpowers are not wholly divorced from reality. But even the manipulators and rulers court disaster when disregard for reality goes beyond certain bounds.

It is with such considerations in mind that one must approach the Nixon-Kissinger doctrine. In Henry Kissinger's view, as explored in these essays, the United States lost its opportunity to dominate the world (or, as he might put it, to construct a stable world order on its own terms) through excessive timidity and misguided moral scruples, nurtured by communist propaganda, with regard to nuclear weapons. The Korean War offered an opportunity to administer a decisive setback to communist power, but it was lost, because the United States feared to apply the strategy of "limited war"—presumably nuclear war, considering the technology of destruction that was in fact employed. As a result of these and other failures, the United States must share power with its imperial rival in a bipolar world order. But, as Brodine and Selden observe, "All of Kissinger's original arguments for limited nuclear war against the Soviet Union now apply to China." In a conflict with China, the logic of the doctrine runs, the U.S. technological advantage might be decisive, if planners are only courageous enough to face the risks.

Nixon and Kissinger are realistically facing the limits of American power when they advocate a return to a more familiar pattern of imperial conquest in Southeast Asia. In the mid-1960s, the United States dispatched an immense expeditionary force to

Indochina. At the peak of involvement, some 800,000 Americans were participating directly in the war, with over 500,000 on the ground. By comparison, recall that the French sent no conscripts to Indochina, and their expeditionary force included 50–60,000 French troops with supporting air and naval forces of perhaps 15,000 men. Recall further that the French were attempting to maintain control of all of Indochina, and of course could not employ a fraction of the firepower available to U.S. forces. The policy of Vietnamization—"the use of mercenaries and of the armies of client regimes in the place of U.S. combat troops," as Buchanan correctly defines it—is a return to a more familiar pattern. At this moment, the United States is employing tens of thousands of mercenaries in the Indochina war, quite apart from the forces of the client regimes for which it provides virtually the sole support in Indochina. The example of Thai troops in Laos, soon to reach perhaps 12,000 according to reliable reports from Vientiane, is a particularly striking example. Not only does the use of Thai mercenaries defy a statute explicitly designed by Congress to prevent just this; furthermore setting Thai and Vietnamese at each others' throats plants the seeds of future conflict that both would surely prefer to avoid.

Similarly, the turn toward more "capital intensive" tactics, with heavier reliance on the technology of surveillance and destruction in place of U.S. ground forces, was a rational return to the principle of comparative advantage: Asian client regimes provide the people to die, while we supply the technology to kill. John Dower points out that the post-Tet strategy, carried further by the Nixon administration, is in many respects a return to the concepts of the 1950s. As Brodine and Selden further explain, the "overall framework of world order" is to remain firmly in U.S. hands, while our partners are to be encouraged to pursue their local interests within the framework of global interests that remains a U.S. monopoly: ". . . other nations are to be recruited to be the cops on the beat. World police headquarters is still to be in Washington."

As for the home front, power must be centralized and insulated from public scrutiny, even from Congress, by the device of executive privilege. Reflecting on this matter, Senator Sam J. Ervin comments: "Throughout history, rulers have imposed secrecy on their actions in order to enslave the citizenry in bonds of ignorance. By contrast, a government whose actions are completely visible to all of its citizens best protects the freedoms embodied in the Constitution." But he fails to add that the "national interest," as defined by those who rule, is best served by secrecy and ignorance.

In the Nixon-Kissinger demonology, the Soviet Union and China are aggressors and outlaws who must be educated in the ways of peace and brought into the international community. Specifically, they must learn not to encourage or support movements for national independence within the global American system, even when these are mass movements that would quickly overthrow client regimes were it not for the direct exercise of American power. In this connection, it is important to stress that Kissinger speaks the language of the ideologist, not that of the historian or political analyst. He does not undertake to elucidate the guiding principles of "the international order" or to justify his claim that, say, China was an aggressor in its border dispute with India, any more than Walt Rostow before him tried to provide historical evidence to support his claim that Stalin incited Ho Chi Minh or the Greek guerrillas.

Similarly, when Kissinger speaks of "limited war," he takes no pains to point out where and why these limited wars are to be fought. It is a central and crucial observation of the essays that follow that Kissinger's "limited wars" are to be fought against the weak on their territory; they are to be fought everywhere in the world where U.S. dominance is challenged, and they are to be fought, if necessary, with nuclear weapons. "Limited wars" are to be further exercises of what Kissinger calls the "judicious application of force" that permitted "American expansion, both economic and geographic," in the past. The same is true of the technology of the "electronic battlefield" and related devices. This is the technology of imperial domination, not great power conflict. American strategists have no illusion of converting Russian territory into an automated murder machine where sensors, computers, "smart bombs," and the like ensure the obedience of the natives.

As the authors observe, Kissinger is willing to "face

up to the risks of Armageddon" and to eschew "avoidance of risk rather than boldness of conception" in the interest of securing the stable world order he envisions. And the President emphasizes that "Potential enemies must know that we will respond to whatever degree is required to protect our interests." More clearly than his adviser, who as a true ideologist prefers the vague and mystical concepts of "stability" and "national interest," the President insists that "economic power will be the key to other kinds of power" and speaks, as he has in the past, of the direct material interests of the United States in Southeast Asia. As to Kissinger's boldness, it has certain advantages for a policy maker. For one thing, he can be assured that he will never be proven wrong in facing the risks of Armageddon. Either the "enemy" will back down and his boldness will have been justified, or they will not, and there will be no one left to pass judgment.

A central purpose of the Nixon-Kissinger strategy for the Pacific is to enlist Japan as a junior partner in maintaining the *status quo*. Here American planners face a quandary, as the authors explain in some detail. There is no guarantee that Japan, having become a powerful military and economic force, may not strike out on its own, for its own "national interest." As Walter LaFeber reminds us, other politicians have "proclaimed that Americans and Japanese should march 'shoulder to shoulder' to develop Asia"; for example, Franklin D. Roosevelt in 1923. In fact, there are ominous similarities between the emerging world order and the international system of the 1930s.

It is clear enough that imperialism is not a spent force. There are unmistakeable signs that the United States is becoming a "mature creditor society," exporting its productive capacity and producing services more than goods, relying on the profits of home-based international corporations to purchase what is produced by cheap and disciplined labor abroad. Furthermore, international sales are becoming a major source of profit for multinational corporations. The IBM Corporation, for example, derived more than 50 percent of its profits through foreign sales in 1970 for the first time in its history, and other major corporations look forward to approaching or passing the "magic 50 percent mark" within a few years (see Brendan Jones, *New York Times,* June 6, 1971). Keith Buchanan comments on the triangular system of the global economy, as the industrial superpowers, the second-level industrial powers, and the colonial societies interact to the continued benefit of the more powerful. For such reasons, the Study Group of the National Planning Association and the Woodrow Wilson Foundation in the early fifties was perceptive, as well as more honest than contemporary ideologists, when it described the primary threat of communism as the economic transformation of the communist powers "in ways which reduce their willingness and ability to complement the industrial economies of the West" (W. Y. Elliot, ed., *Political Economy of American Foreign Policy,* 1955,

p. 42). And if the "developing nations" choose at some point to use their own resources for their own purposes, or to carry out internal social change in ways which will reduce their contributions to the industrial economies of the West (and Japan), these imperial powers must be prepared to employ sufficient force to prevent such unreasonable behavior, which will no doubt be described as "internal aggression" and blamed on the most plausible "enemy" of the day. It is not only the developing nations that must be controlled in such ways. At a very different level of imperial dominance, British auto workers must not be permitted to demand economic benefits or a share in management control in the Ford plant and must be subject to threats that can be wielded quite effectively by an international corporation. Such problems will be particularly acute in East Asia, a region which many regard as most promising for the "internationalization of production" and for supplying raw materials for the insatiable industrial powers. This is the general context within which one must interpret the Nixon-Kissinger plans for a stable world order incorporating as much of East Asia as possible, and in particular, their commitment to achieving a Korea-type solution in Vietnam.

But if imperialism is not a spent force, neither is resistance to imperial aggression. The Vietnamese resistance of the past quarter-century is a historical event of first magnitude. The U.S. executive apparently still hopes to grind down the resistance "by sheer weight and mass" (in the words of nation builder Robert Komer). But the resistance in Indo-china maintains its astonishing resilience. It is an important fact that it has awakened some segments of American society to a civilized response, to protest and domestic resistance. The Vietnamese struggle for national liberation has led to a loss of confidence in the leading imperial power, a matter that is duly noted and deplored by imperial ideologists and that may have important consequences outside of East Asia as well. Peter Wiles notes that "An imperialist government has to feel a great historic righteousness about what it does . . .; *imperialist remorse* . . . is the basis of imperialist decline." The remark is exaggerated, but it contains a kernel of truth. The American war in Indochina has shattered the image of historic righteousness. It has, furthermore, somewhat diminished the superiority in force and economic power that permitted the United States to intervene in the internal affairs of others. For such reasons, the courageous struggle of the Vietnamese might, conceivably, prove to be a turning point in modern history.

The authors offer a note of hope. They believe that the American people are committed to withdrawal from Vietnam, and that peace in Vietnam may be "the first step toward returning to the American people a voice in their own destiny." Is such optimism warranted? Readers of this book, and their fellow citizens, will determine, by their actions, the answer to this question.

I

HENRY KISSINGER'S DIPLOMACY OF FORCE

A Foreign Policy Roundtable Paper

VIRGINIA BRODINE AND MARK SELDEN

The Foreign Policy Roundtable is an informal group, most of whose members are on the Washington University faculty in St. Louis. The Roundtable initiated the cooperative study with members of the University of California (Berkeley) faculty which led to the publication of The Politics of Escalation, a Citizens' White Paper, *by Franz Schurmann, Peter Dale Scott, and Reginald Zelnik. The Roundtable also arranged a national conference,* United States Involvement in Thailand *in May 1967 which brought together anthropologists, historians, and others who had special knowledge of Thailand for an intensive inquiry into U.S.-Thailand relations.*

Virginia Brodine was Editor of Environment *for seven years until 1969 and is presently Consulting Editor. She is the author of a forthcoming book on air pollution. Mark Selden is Assistant Professor of History at Washington University. He is the editor (with Edward Friedman) of* America's Asia, Dissenting Essays on Asian-American Relations *and a coeditor of the* Bulletin of Concerned Asian Scholars. *He is the author of* The Yenan Way in Revolutionary China.

A policy completely at odds with the will and the interests of the majority of the people is guiding the actions of this country in Vietnam, resulting in a failure of trust between the people and the President. A policy gap and a credibility gap of these dimensions represents an intolerable situation in a democracy. The vast majority of the American people want out of the war in Indochina now. Mr. Nixon has been saying since the 1968 campaign that he wants to end the war, too. At one time he said "we will end the war before the end of 1970." Yet it continues.[1] The people can no longer believe the President when he talks about the war. In spite of present hope of a new era in Sino-U.S. relations, the failure of trust makes it impossible for the people to accept at face

[1] The President's "end the war before the end of 1970" statement was made at a press conference in the fall of 1969. See *Department of State Bulletin,* October 13, 1969. In February 1971, the Gallup Poll asked the following question: "A proposal has been made in Congress to require the U.S. government to bring home all U.S. troops from Vietnam before the end of this year. Would you like to have your Congressman vote for or against this proposal?" Of those queried, 66 percent were for the proposal. At the same time, the Poll asked: "Do you think the Nixon administration is or is not telling the public all they should know about the Vietnam War?" Of those queried, 69 percent thought the administration was not telling the public all they should know. Late in 1971, a Harris poll found 65 percent believing the Vietnam War morally wrong.

value the President's characterization of his journey to China as a step toward peace "not just for our generation but for future generations."

The credibility gap arises in part from deliberate withholding of information. Nixon's Assistant for National Security Affairs, Henry A. Kissinger, justifies the secrecy about Southeast Asian policy with an analogy to a chess game:

If you see two people playing chess and someone comes along and says, "Why don't you make this move?" you're in an impossible position. You can't answer. You can't tell your chess opponent your game plan. This attempt to get peace in Vietnam may involve 15 or 18 moves. It is a tragedy of the democratic process. Critics, perfectly legitimately, raise questions. But we're in the difficult position of not being able to answer.[2]

But we have not just happened along to watch a game. We have the uncomfortable feeling that we, the American people, are the pawns on the chess board.

If we are *not* to be pawns, what we need to know is not the single move the administration will make next in Indochina or what proposals Mr. Nixon and Dr. Kissinger have made to China, but what strategy is guiding their "game plan." Whether the move toward China is seen as part of the Vietnam "game" or as a different game being played simultaneously on another chessboard, the strategy arises from the

[2] Henry A. Kissinger, quoted by G. Astor in *Look,* August 12, 1969.

same conception of foreign policy and is being prepared in the same secrecy. We need to know the nature of the policy which has brought repeated extensions of the war geographically, repeated intensifications militarily. We need to know whether the approach to China envisions an Asian peace that is to the mutual advantage of the United States, Indochina, China, and other Asian nations, or involves a dangerous diplomatic "game" with an uncertain outcome. This paper represents a search for the answer to these questions. They are profoundly serious questions, not only for the immediate and urgent issues of today, but also for the still unforeseen foreign policy issues of coming months and years. Moreover, as the policy gap and the credibility gap between the President and the people widen and deepen, the erosion of democracy this represents threatens to become irreparable.

The course of recent history might have been different had the people of this country known *at the time* they were made, about the decisions in the Eisenhower administration to prevent the reunification elections in Vietnam called for by the Geneva Agreement; in the Kennedy administration to institute sabotage in North Vietnam and intervention in Laos; in the Johnson administration to create pretexts for escalating the war. Now these crucial decisions and the efforts to keep them from the people have been revealed in the *Pentagon Papers*.[3] But we cannot wait

[3] *The Pentagon Papers,* the Senator Gravel edition, 4 vols. (Boston: Beacon Press, 1971).

five or ten years for the story of the Nixon administration's decision making. Too many lives—American
and Indochinese—will be lost if the war continues
five or ten *months,* while present decisions may be
leading to new escalations and even to the brink
of nuclear war.

The policy of the Nixon administration is not really
secret. Stripped of its rhetoric, the outlines clearly
emerge. But only by going back to its origins in the
preadministration writings of its principal architect,
Dr. Kissinger, can its truly dangerous implications
be understood.

To look for the basis of present policy in Kissinger's
writings is not to suggest that he, *rather than Nixon,*
is making policy. The Kissinger-Nixon Doctrine bears
the Nixon as well as the Kissinger stamp, particularly
as it relates to Asia. It was foreshadowed in Nixon's
prepresidential speeches and especially in his article
in *Foreign Affairs* in 1967. What must have been
most attractive to Nixon in Kissinger's ideas was
their correspondence with many of his own.[4] It was
not necessary for Kissinger to win Nixon over to a

[4] Although Kissinger's first government service was as a
consultant to the Democratic administration of John F. Kennedy, and he was also policy adviser to Nelson Rockefeller
during the 1968 campaign, it is interesting that he had a good
word to say for Nixon as early as 1958. When asked about
"men in public life whom you admire and look to for leadership" he responded, "I think that Mr. Nixon in his public
utterances lately has shown an awareness of the situation."
Mike Wallace asked the question in an interview originally
published by the Fund for the Republic in 1958 and recently
reprinted as "Second Edition/Limited War," in *The Center
Magazine,* 4, No. 1 (January–February 1971).

new view of world affairs, only to a particular way of manipulating them.

In none of his five books does Kissinger give more than passing mention to the role of the people in a democracy in determining foreign policy. At one point he asks, "What is the future of democracy when the propagandistic side of politics becomes more and more separated from the substantive side?"[5] Although he provides no answer, he claims that "The democracies which have been most successful have been those based on essentially aristocratic forms"[6] and talks about the advantages of aristocracy in making foreign policy as opposed to the danger of "egalitarian" or "plebiscitarian" democracy. His concern lies with effective leadership, which he says must "define purposes perhaps only vaguely apprehended by the multitude."[7]

Kissinger has been severely critical of past leadership and policy-making structure in the United States; critical of the timidity of the governmental bureaucracy, of the proliferation of government committees which he says have a "pernicious" effect on policy; critical of the failure to integrate political and military structures and policies.

Two weeks after Nixon's inauguration, the new President took the first steps to create a policy-

[5] *The Necessity for Choice* (New York: Harper & Row, 1960), p. 322.

[6] Ibid., p. 313.

[7] *Nuclear Weapons and Foreign Policy* (New York: Harper & Row, 1957), p. 431.

making apparatus that would meet Kissinger's requirements.[8] The National Security Council staff, which Kissinger now directs, channels all policy information and proposals for alternative courses of action through Kissinger directly to the President. It carries still further the tendency in recent administrations toward freeing the executive from congressional influences and restraints in the foreign policy field. It now numbers more than forty professionals, plus supporting staff. In addition, it draws on the Joint Chiefs of Staff, the Department of State, and the Department of Defense for studies and opinions. Many of the important foreign policy committees are firmly under Kissinger's control. For example, he chairs the committee which reviews the studies of foreign policy alternatives, as well as the Vietnam Special Studies Group and the Defense Program Review Committee. The Washington Special Action Group which deals with crises like the Cambodian invasion is chaired by the President, with Kissinger as a member. In November 1971, Kissinger's grip on foreign policy was further strengthened when a National Security Council Intelligence Committee was set up under his chairmanship.

One of the purposes of this apparatus is to insulate the President from interagency squabbles. No doubt it succeeds. It also insulates the President from the

[8] Foreign Affairs Manual Circular No. 521, February 6, 1969 and White House Announcement, February 7, 1969; *Department of State Bulletin,* February 24, 1969, pp. 163–166.

vigorous personal presentation of any point of view except Kissinger's until the time to make a final decision. Only Secretary of State Rogers and Secretary of Defense Laird have regular access to the President on foreign policy matters outside the National Security Council system, and even they lack Kissinger's daily contact with the President. The system also insulates the policy-making process from the advice and consent of the Senate, for although representatives of the Departments of State and Defense testify before congressional committees, the entire NSC apparatus and the man at its head—Kissinger—are unavailable to Congress.

The system provides a structure for integrating the threat and use of force with the practice of diplomacy, one of the basic tenets of the Kissinger method. Indeed, foreign policy has now become indistinguishable from national security affairs.

The Doctrine that has emerged from the National Security apparatus under Kissinger and Nixon is not a creative new doctrine based on the realities of the seventies, although Nixon likes to present it that way. As John Dower shows in another essay in this book, it is in many ways the same old policy that led us into Indochina in the first place, but with some particularly dangerous aspects. It is not a doctrine based on the formation of peaceful relationships with China and the nations of Southeast Asia growing out of a settlement of the Indochina War, but one that leads to the continuation of that war and that plants the seeds of new ones. The Cambodian and Laotian invasions were logical outcomes of the Doctrine, and the grave danger remains of other and sharper escalations.

There are only a few escalations still possible before the limits of conventional war are reached. Implicit in each of them is not only the probability of bringing greater power in on the other side, but also, in spite of the recent improvement in U.S.-China relations, a serious risk of war with China or the USSR. Furthermore, an analysis of the strategic conceptions Kissinger has developed over the years suggests that if a settlement is not reached by the time these "options" are exhausted, the next step might involve the use of nuclear weapons, disclaimers by Nixon and Kissinger to the contrary notwithstanding.

DR. KISSINGER'S WORLD ORDER

Kissinger was first heard from in the late fifties, preaching a lesson from history: the lesson that total peace was impossible, but that international stability might be attainable. His first book, *A World Restored,* dealt with Europe in the decade 1812–1822, and from that period he extracted a universal principle:

Those ages which in retrospect seem most peaceful were least in search of peace. Those whose quest for it seems unending appear least able to achieve tranquility. Whenever peace—conceived as the avoidance of war—has been the primary objective of a power or a group of powers, the international system has been at the mercy of the most ruthless member of the international community. Whenever the international order has acknowledged that certain principles could not be compromised even for the sake of peace, stability based on an equilibrium of forces was at least conceivable.[9]

The pursuit of international stability—not the pursuit of peace—has been the central theme around which Kissinger has constructed his grand design for United States foreign policy ever since.

Before accepting the application of his nineteenth-century lesson to our own period, it is worth examining a little more closely. Has he really found a universal principle that applies throughout history? We might check its universality by trying to apply it to another period. Take the age of *Pax Romana*, for example, when Roman armies maintained imperial power from Britain to the Mideast. Would Kissinger consider *that* an age when stability was based on an equilibrium of forces, and the international system was not at the mercy of its most ruthless member? There is only one oblique reference in Kissinger's work to the Roman Empire, in which he calls it "a peaceful *status quo* power." Kissinger recognizes that the road to unchallenged imperial supremacy was not a peaceful one. "It was, after all, no consolation for Carthage that 150 years after its destruction Rome was transformed into a peaceful *status quo* power."[10] The road to U.S. supremacy was not completely peaceful, either, but he puts that a little differently. ". . . American expansion,

[9] *A World Restored* (London: Weidenfeld & Nicolson, 1957), p. 1.
[10] *The Necessity for Choice*, p. 300.

both economic and geographic, was not accomplished without a judicious application of force."[11]

As Dr. Kissinger continued to write out his diagnosis of what ailed American foreign policy and to prescribe a new regimen, what he recommended sounded much like a *Pax Americana*. As the underlying purpose of pursuing international stability emerged, it was revealed as a world order based on U.S. supremacy rather than on a nineteenth-century equilibrium.

What Kissinger himself saw as the important parallel with the past was the instability of our own day and that of 1812, both created by what he calls "revolutionary" powers—Napoleonic France and, in our time, the Soviet Union and China. They are revolutionary not simply because they have had internal revolutions, but because they refuse "to accept the framework of the international order or the domestic structure of other states, or both."

International order in the nineteenth century was restored, according to Kissinger, by the military defeat of the revolutionary power and the reestablishment of stability based on what he calls "legitimacy." This legitimacy has nothing to do with justice or morality or the well-being of the people within a nation. Nor is it necessarily legal, for the central legitimizing principle that embodies it may not be written down in any international agreement. It simply means that a group of nations have a similar approach to the "permissible aims and methods of

[11] *Nuclear Weapons and Foreign Policy*, p. 427.

foreign policy" and act on a similar understanding of what "cannot be compromised even for the sake of peace." Kissinger describes how this principle was defined under the leadership of Metternich. "When the unity of Europe came to pass, it was through a cynical use of the conference machinery to define a legitimizing principle of social repression."

From that time until the outbreak of World War I Europe enjoyed stability. There were revolutions, it is true, but they were suppressed; there were wars, but they were limited.

Kissinger's vision, then, is a world order under American leadership that will restore stability to the twentieth-century world; peace may not reign, but revolutions will be suppressed and wars will be limited.

When he wrote *Nuclear Weapons and Foreign Policy* (1957), the same first step as in the previous century seemed in order: the military defeat of the revolutionary power, the Soviet Union, or its restraint under the threat of military defeat. Kissinger regretted that the best opportunity had already gone by—the period of our atomic monopoly and the following years of overwhelming nuclear superiority. The U.S. then, he says "underestimated the bargaining power inherent in our industrial potential and our nuclear superiority." This "failure" he attributes to the "ban the bomb" campaign and other "Soviet propaganda" moves which "almost imperceptibly shifted the primary concern away from Soviet aggression—the real security problem—to the immorality of the use of nuclear weapons which happened to represent the most effective means for resisting it."[12]

With that opportunity gone, and Soviet nuclear power increasing, he recognized that there could be no victor in an all-out nuclear war. It was no longer useful even to threaten massive retaliation because to carry out the threat would be suicidal. The Soviet Union could respond in kind. Nevertheless, credible threats must be developed, productive strategies must be worked out, for, according to Kissinger, world order can only be achieved and maintained by a combination of diplomacy and force. Force without diplomacy is "immoderate in triumph and panicky in adversity,"[13] but "diplomacy which is not related to a plausible employment of force is sterile."[14]

Not that he ever advocates abandoning a capability for all-out war. It is essential, he says, to recognize the necessity for all-out war capability, but also its limits. It "can only avert disaster. It cannot be employed to achieve positive ends."[15] What can be employed to achieve positive ends are "concepts of war which bring power into balance with the willingness to use it."[16] In 1957 he advocated a concept of war which he called limited, but which could include nuclear weapons ranging all the way up to 500 kilotons —more than 20 times the explosive power of the Hiroshima bomb.

[12] *Nuclear Weapons and Foreign Policy*, p. 376.
[13] *A World Restored*, p. 125.
[14] *Nuclear Weapons and Foreign Policy*, p. 201.
[15] Ibid., p. 131.
[16] Ibid., p. 26.

The concepts of war he has developed since have changed little except that for situations short of all-out war, he has lowered his nuclear ceiling, and in more recent books, limits his advocacy to the use of *tactical* nuclear weapons. A one-kiloton tactical weapon, "small" as nuclear weapons go, has 500 times the explosive force of the World War II block-buster, a two-ton TNT bomb. Some tactical weapons are only a fraction of a kiloton, but as their yield increases, the point at which tactical weapons stop and strategic weapons begin is difficult, if not impossible, to define. The difference between limiting nuclear war to weapons no larger than 500 kilotons and limiting nuclear war to tactical weapons may therefore be more apparent than real.

International stability requires, in Kissinger's view, not only the force to defeat or contain a revolutionary power, but also a legitimizing principle around which world order can be developed. Social repression was the legitimizing principle in the Metternich period, he says, national self-determination that of the period between the two world wars, but he never makes explicit his legitimizing principle for the contemporary world. Preventing the spread of communism is the principle implied in his early books, but in 1968 he rejects this definition. "Our goal," he says, "should be to build a moral consensus" among many noncommunist nations.[17] Yet he states no moral principle

[17] *American Foreign Policy, Three Essays* (New York: W. W. Norton & Co., 1969), p. 84.

which might serve to build this consensus, and continues to call for a foreign policy determined by concepts of power and equilibrium. He says that "our concept of world order must have deeper purposes than stability"[18] but never elucidates these deeper purposes.

In the period immediately following World War II, U.S. power expanded tremendously around the world. As the old imperialist powers, defeated or weakened in the war and opposed by vigorous anticolonialist movements, pulled out, U.S. economic and military penetration spread rapidly throughout Asia and elsewhere. The expansion and consolidation of this power were carried out in the name of preventing the spread of communism. When Kissinger began to write, he accepted this global U.S. power as given, the U.S. as a *status quo* power, whose problem was the maintenance of that power. "As a *status quo* power, the basic strategic problem for the United States is to be clear about what strategic transformations we are prepared to resist,"[19] he said, although there was also the problem of how to "bring about strategic changes favorable to our side."[20]

He still sees it that way. True, by the late sixties, Kissinger recognized that the U.S. must share some of the power and some of the military tasks within particular regions with other nations. Not, however,

---

[18] Ibid., p. 94.
[19] *Nuclear Weapons and Foreign Policy*, p. 8.
[20] Ibid., p. 147.

the "overall framework of order," which remains in U.S. hands.[21]

Kissinger's "legitimizing principle" boils down to nothing more nor less than the defense of the *status quo*. He wants to legitimize the defense of the *status quo* within third world countries (or the replacement of unstable governments with more stable ones) because "A stable domestic system in the new countries will not automatically produce international order, but international order is impossible without it."[22] He wants to legitimize the perpetuation of U.S. power around the world, for this is the real heart of his world order, whether it is seen in the world of 1957, with the U.S. almost alone, confronting a monolithic communism, or in the world of 1969, with the U.S. as the global leader of a collection of regional alliances. It is perhaps not surprising that he finds it, after all, impossible to spell out a legitimizing principle capable of rallying other nations behind the maintenance of U.S. supremacy. (Nixon may appeal to the people of this country for sacrifices in the name of remaining "Number One" but this rallying cry hardly appeals beyond U.S. borders.)

Most revealing of Kissinger's approach to world order are his models. The British Empire, in its heyday as a *status quo* power, had what he calls a "precautionary" defensive strategy, meaning that protective action is taken against the *capability* of a threat, without waiting for the threat to become overt.

[21] *American Foreign Policy*, p. 97.
[22] Ibid., p. 84.

". . . British policy was based on the proposition that by the time the opponent's intentions were clear, it was too late to affect them."[23] So with the U.S. in the latter half of the twentieth century: "The Soviet strategy of ambiguity can ultimately be countered only by a policy of precaution, by attempting to nip Soviet moves in the bud."[24] This kind of policy he sees as especially necessary now, because "In the nuclear age, by the time a threat has become unambiguous it may be too late to resist it."[25]

There was also that great Empire technique of "showing the flag," so effective with less powerful countries. A British ship simply sailed into the harbor of a potential trouble-making nation, with the Union Jack flying. The power behind that symbol was very well known, and the implicit threat was sometimes adequate for British purposes. What the U.S. needs, Kissinger suggested in 1957, was "a twentieth-century equivalent of 'showing the flag,' an ability and a readiness to make our power felt quickly and decisively, not only to deter Soviet aggression but also to impress the uncommitted with our capacity for decisive action."[26]

Another model is past U.S. policy in the Western Hemisphere. In explaining that the concept of limited war is really not new to us, he points out that "Every

[23] *Problems of National Strategy, A Book of Readings*, Editor's Introduction (New York: Frederick A. Praeger, 1965), p. 3.
[24] *Nuclear Weapons and Foreign Policy*, p. 334.
[25] Ibid., p. 9.
[26] Ibid., p. 264.

war in which we have been engaged in the Western Hemisphere was a limited war," and notes that these wars have been not only frequent, but "productive."[27] He doesn't list them, but there have been literally hundreds. To mention just a few of these "productive" wars, there were the Mexican War and the Spanish-American War, both of which added territory to the U.S., the occupation of Nicaragua by U.S. Marines (1912–1933), and the overthrow of the Guatemalan government in 1954, which made these countries safe for United Fruit. More recently and less productively, there was the Bay of Pigs expedition against Cuba.

In his early writing, Kissinger is brutally frank about the use of American power to achieve American dominance. The manner rather than the matter changes in later years. He always has a preference for gaining American ends with a warning rather than a war if possible, but the warning must always be backed up by the capability and the willingness to go to war if warnings are inadequate.

On the eve of his move from Harvard to the White House, he recognized that the methods of the cold war period, like its language, would no longer do. While the United States still "disposes of the greatest single aggregate of material power in the world" this "inescapable" fact of international life can no longer work in quite the simple way it did in the two decades after 1945 when, so Kissinger says, we assumed that this power, along with technology

[27] Ibid., pp. 136–137.

and managerial skills gave us the ability to "reshape the international system and to bring about domestic transformations in 'emerging countries.'" He perceived as the new challenge "to evoke the creativity of a pluralistic world, to base order on political multipolarity even though overwhelming military strength will remain with the two superpowers."[28]

Yet the change in Kissinger's scheme is not really from bipolarity to multipolarity; the superpower USA is to remain dominant, though lesser countries are to have new responsibilities. A decade before the term "Vietnamization" was coined, Kissinger had already stated the importance of building up indigenous regional defenses, while maintaining U.S. ascendancy in determining when and where to fight. We needed an effective system of alliances built around a "strategy of local defense and a diplomacy of regional cooperation" but "the United States alone of the powers in the non-Soviet world is strong enough physically and psychologically to play a global role," and ". . . the responsibility for defining the issues for which to contend has explicitly fallen on us."[29]

He sees this conception as still valid for the seventies, when "our role will be to contribute to a structure that will foster the initiative of others. . . . Our contribution should not be the sole or principal effort, but it should make the difference between success and failure."[30] Which is to say, if Suharto appears to

[28] *American Foreign Policy*, pp. 57–58.
[29] *Nuclear Weapons and Foreign Policy*, pp. 250, 252.
[30] *American Foreign Policy*, pp. 93–94.

be losing his grip on Indonesia, or if the Lon Nol
government of Cambodia takes an initiative against
North Vietnam, but can't sustain it alone, the U.S.
will "make the difference between success and failure." As the financial and political costs of U.S. forces
fighting Asian land wars becomes prohibitive the
U.S. will insure that some Asians have the means to
fight other Asians. Kissinger's emphasis on involving
other noncommunist nations in supporting U.S. interests in their own region has certain clear limits.
Their role must be *restricted to that region.* "Outside
that region we must be free to act alone or with a
different grouping of powers if our interest so dic-
tates."[31] For example, although he believes the U.S.
should allow the Western European nations more
freedom of action and responsibility vis-à-vis Eastern
European nations, he suggests that Western dealings
with the Soviet Union should be a U.S. responsibility.[32] Asian allies in the Kissinger view should
have nothing to say about U.S. dealings with Europe,
nor should European nations be allowed to interfere
with our conduct of a war in Asia.

According to Kissinger we made the mistake of
allowing such interference at the time of the Korean
War. We should not have brought our European allies into it at all. We did not really need their help,
and they were concerned with "the risk, however
slight, that the Korean War might spread to Europe."
They were therefore very cautious and inhibited the

[31] *Nuclear Weapons and Foreign Policy,* p. 250.
[32] *American Foreign Policy,* p. 78.

U.S. from such action as hot pursuit of enemy planes into China, or other, even more decisive action. Yet the U.S. should have been concerned with the "strategic opportunities" the war offered to administer a setback to China. As Kissinger saw it, the opportunities were worth the risk that this could be done without bringing China's ally, the USSR, into the conflict and setting off an all-out war.[33]

By the same token, what we do in Indochina should not be affected by the fact that the war is "highly unpopular in many countries." It is important to the U.S. global position to prove its "steadiness" and military competence, for "Even critics are unlikely to be reassured by a complete collapse of the American effort in Vietnam."[34]

Kissinger recognizes that there are many difficulties in the way of building his world order. The leaders of the new nations "feel little sense of responsibility to an over-all international equilibrium; they are much more conscious of their local grievances."[35] They may be susceptible to the influence of China or the Soviet Union. Indeed, by 1968 he finds "intervention in the third world" by these two countries, more than direct aggression, to be among the "concrete issues which threaten peace."[36]

The foreign policies of the third world nations, he says, "are often cast in an anti-Western mold be-

[33] *Nuclear Weapons and Foreign Policy,* pp. 52–53.
[34] *American Foreign Policy,* p. 112.
[35] Ibid., p. 80.
[36] Ibid., p. 90.

cause this is the easiest way to recreate the struggle against imperial rule which is the unifying element for new nations."[37] Although he advocates developing "shared purposes" with these nations, this expression scarcely conceals his colonialist bias. Speaking as if Western imperialism has passed from the world completely, he sums up its passing with this tribute: "It was the *moral success* of the imperial powers which undermined their political rule."[38] (Kissinger's emphasis.)

Kissinger's analysis, in 1968 as in 1957, places the United States in the position of global gendarme. Not only must it actively guard against "instability" —intervening to prevent revolutionary change everywhere—but it should also adopt a forward posture to preempt the possibilities of aggression by such nations as China and Russia whose very existence poses a threat to U.S. hegemony. Where this has led can be seen by looking at the foreign policy of the Nixon administration, of which Kissinger is the principal architect.

The Nixon administration came into office with a stated commitment to "move from an era of confrontation to an era of negotiation,"[39] and to accept "sufficiency" in arms, rather than the large margin of

[37] Ibid., p. 41.

[38] *Necessity for Choice*, p. 320.

[39] This phrase appeared in Nixon's inaugural address and has been repeated many times since, for example, on March 14, 1969, when he announced the deployment of the ABM "Safeguard" System. *Department of State Bulletin*, 60:274, March 31, 1969.

superiority over the USSR that had been the goal of
U.S. arms policy for a quarter of a century.[40] There
were also indications of a willingness to take a new
look at U.S. policy toward China and a plan (unspecified) for ending the war in Vietnam. Was this a
creative response to the challenge of the new multi-
polar world and to the growing desire of the American people for peace in Vietnam? Hardly. By the
end of the administration's first year in office it had
become clear that the arms race would continue.[41]
In Nixon's commencement address to the Air Force
Academy on June 4, 1969, he spelled out his guiding
principle in defense spending as to err "on the side
of too much" rather than on the side of too little.[42]
Only if the Soviet Union would cut its help to North

[40] Although "sufficiency" sounds much more moderate than
"superiority" it was never intended to mean "parity," and in
fact is a very elastic conception. As the President explained it
at a news conference on February 6, 1969: "I would say, with
regard to Dr. Kissinger's suggestion of sufficiency, that that
would meet certainly my guideline, and, I think, Secretary
Laird's guideline with regard to superiority. . . . Our objective
is to be sure that the United States has sufficient military
power to defend our interests and to maintain the commitments which this administration determines are in the interest of the United States around the world. I think 'sufficiency' is a better term, actually, than either 'superiority'
or 'parity.' " *Department of State Bulletin* 60:143, February 17,
1969.

[41] Strategic Arms Limitations Talks had already been agreed
upon between the U.S. and the USSR and preliminary work
done by the Johnson administration, but Kissinger and Nixon
took another six months to prepare, meanwhile moving to deploy an Antiballistic Missile (ABM) system and test multiple
independent reentry vehicles (MIRV). *Department of State
Bulletin* 60:527, June 23, 1969.

[42] Ibid.

Vietnam, pressure Hanoi to accept U.S. terms for ending the conflict, or make concessions in other areas of tension would the U.S. look favorably on a reduction of armaments.[43] In spite of diplomatic overtures to China, the administration's Asian policy was to be based on military alliances with reactionary Asian governments, bolstered with U.S. military bases all around China's periphery. And finally, the plan to end the war in Vietnam, while it did not call for unconditional surrender nevertheless made it clear that victory remained the U.S. goal.

[43] This much is clear from the public record. For example in a commencement address at Emerson College, June 8, 1969, Undersecretary of State Elliot Richardson said that Nixon's "too much rather than too little" principle "does not mean that we must be backed forever into an upward spiral of arms expenditures." He said the key to unlocking this spiral and reversing its direction would be found in what Nixon had called "specific moves to reduce tensions around the world." Richardson continued: "The point of departure for any such move is a specific situation of tension, one which breeds conflict and holds a significant risk of confrontation between the Soviet Union and ourselves. The Middle East is one such situation. Viet-Nam is another. Berlin access is a third." *Department of State Bulletin* 60:560, June 30, 1969.

Whether there was any private effort to bargain with the Soviet Union for help in achieving a Vietnam solution and if so, what was offered, can only be guessed at. In any event, it seems that if such efforts were made, they were unsuccessful. In his 1970 "State of the World" message, Nixon chided the USSR in these terms: "Our overall relationship with the USSR remains far from satisfactory. To the detriment of the cause of peace, the Soviet leadership has failed to exert a helpful influence over the North Vietnamese in Paris. The overwhelming majority of the war materiel that reaches North Vietnam comes from the USSR which thereby bears a heavy responsibility for the continuation of this war. This cannot but cloud the rest of our relationship with the Soviet Union." *Department of State Bulletin*, 62:325, March 9, 1970.

In fact, as the guiding doctrine took shape in words and action, it became more and more obvious that it was built to the Kissinger specifications for world order. The most complete expression of the Kissinger-Nixon Doctrine is in Nixon's "State of the World" message to Congress on February 25, 1971.[44] There are the concepts (often expressed in only slightly different words) of Kissinger's previous writings, along with the Nixon emphasis on the U.S. as a Pacific power. There is a recognition of some of the changes that have taken place on the international scene since the end of World War II, and particularly in recent years. These include the growing military might of the USSR, the recovery and now the "economic vitality" of Western Europe and Japan, and the rise of new nations now able to "shoulder more responsibility for their own security and well-being." The breakup of the communist bloc is noted, particularly the conflict between the Soviet Union and China which "presents different challenges and new opportunities." All these have led to

. . . a new era of multilateral diplomacy. . . . It is an increasingly heterogeneous and complex world, and the dangers of local conflict are multiplied. But so, too are the opportunities for creative diplomacy.

Perhaps in preparation for this creative diplomacy, the tone of voice is lower than it used to be. As Nixon said on another occasion, "I know that what is called cold-war rhetoric isn't fashionable these

[44] Ibid., 64:342–432, March 22, 1971.

days and I am not engaging in it, because I am quite practical."[45] But those who listen closely hear the quieter voices saying many of the old things.

The long-term goal of the U.S. is explained as what Kissinger has long advocated—a new system of international stability. The "new" system is to be based on the network of bilateral, multilateral, and regional commitments constructed during the cold war to "contain" China and insure U.S. global hegemony. The threat of U.S. nuclear retaliation is to be kept alive should U.S. interests be challenged anywhere. There is a tactical change involving the substitution of American materiel and technology and the troops of other nations for American ground troops (and in Western Europe even this change does not apply —there was to be no reduction in U.S. ground troops there). Nixon and Kissinger have recognized the immense financial and political costs of a strategy based on a large input of U.S. ground forces, but propose no other reductions in U.S. global commitments.

International stability is still to be based on U.S. military and economic power with Western Europe and Japan as junior—if increasingly powerful—partners and other noncommunist allies as lesser members of the firm. There is also some talk of bringing communist nations into a "balanced international structure." Yet, in the words of the message, Cuba "excludes itself" and "In certain fundamental aspects," (as Kissinger has been saying since the fifties)

45 Ibid., 63:105, July 27, 1970.

"the Soviet outlook on world affairs is incompatible with a stable international system." Dialogue with China is advocated as long as it is not "at the expense of international order or our own commitments." The world described in the message is still a divided, and therefore an inherently unstable world.

There are indications that communist nations have interests which noncommunist nations must respect. In East Asia, four major powers: Japan, the Soviet Union, the People's Republic of China, and the United States are said to require adjustment of their policies to the legitimate interests of the others. Here is obviously an important theater for "creative diplomacy," but the hints of change are meager.

The peace that is promised continues to sound much like a *Pax Americana*. Although U.S. global supremacy is not flaunted as it was in the fifties the system restricts the influence of the junior partners to their own regions, while that of the U.S. is worldwide. If the role of the United States as world policeman is to be limited, as Nixon has said,[46] the difference is that other nations are to be recruited to be the cops on the beat. World police headquarters is still to be in Washington.

Moreover, the Doctrine is not at all incomptaible with war. In fact, were the U.S. not already involved in a war, there would have been a serious danger, under the Doctrine, that we soon would become so involved. As it is, the strategy that is an integral part

[46] Richard M. Nixon, "Asia after Viet Nam," *Foreign Affairs,* 46 (October 1967): 124.

of the Doctrine shapes the course of that war. The Doctrine stands on two legs: the strategic concepts of Henry Kissinger, and Richard Nixon's long involvement with Asian policy and particularly with his war in Indochina—for it is his war, just as much as it was once Johnson's war.

MR. NIXON'S WAR

As senator, vice president, and then as the leader of the Republican party, Nixon made many foreign policy statements before he became President. Like Kissinger, he has an historical lesson for us:

The lesson of all history warns us that we should negotiate only when our military superiority is so convincing that we can achieve our objective at the conference table—and deny the aggressors theirs.[47]

This conviction has permeated his approach to foreign policy throughout his career.

As the focus of American foreign policy preoccupations has shifted, Nixon's tone toward the Soviet Union has gradually changed from the 1953 advocacy of rolling back Soviet power[48] to a 1967 statement that its "westward advance" has been "contained."[49] On Asia, however, Nixon has been remarkably consistent. One aspect of this consistency on Asia was

[47] Richard M. Nixon, "Why Not Negotiate in Vietnam," *The Reader's Digest* (December 1965), p. 51.
[48] Quoted by D. F. Fleming in *The Cold War and its Origins* (New York: Doubleday and Company, 1961), p. 740.
[49] "Asia after Viet Nam," p. 124.

noted rather acidly by the *New York Times* in its lead editorial, April 18, 1971:

Seventeen years ago, Vice President Richard M. Nixon, speaking before the American Society of Newspaper Editors, sent up his famous trial balloon proposing that if necessary American ground troops be employed in Indochina to prevent a Commuist takeover there. Seventeen years to the day and 44,000 American deaths later, President Richard M. Nixon, speaking before the American Society of Newspaper Editors, made it clear that American troops will not be totally withdrawn from Indochina until one part of that country—namely, South Vietnam—has developed "the capacity to defend [itself] against a Communist take-over." *Plus ça change* . . .

On basic foreign policy issues, it is hard to find any important differences in the views of Kissinger and Nixon before they joined forces. They agreed on the maintenance of U.S. global power with force if necessary, on unremitting hostility to the two communist giants, on resistance to revolutions from the left in other countries, and on U.S. supremacy in the nuclear arms race—the principal strands of hard-line anticommunist cold war foreign policy.

There were differences in rhetoric. Kissinger prefers the cold-blooded statement of national interest; Nixon, the moral justification. While Kissinger was warning that we could no longer afford to "confine our actions to situations in which our moral, legal and military positions are completely in harmony" but must have a policy that presupposes "a willingness to run risks on partial knowledge and for a less than perfect application of one's principles,"[50] Nixon was declaiming that "an attack on freedom anywhere is an attack on freedom everywhere" and "our moral position is right."[51]

On the other hand, one would never know from reading Kissinger that the U.S. had an *economic* interest anywhere in the world, while Nixon, arguing that we must oppose communism in Southeast Asia, emphasizes Malaysia's rubber and tin[52] and the "immense mineral potential" of Indonesia, "the region's richest hoard of natural resources"[53] which must not be allowed to fall into communist hands.

There were differences in strategy and differences in focus: Nixon supported the Dulles strategy of massive retaliation when Kissinger was developing his strategy of limited war.[54] A great deal of Kissinger's writing is focused on Europe, while Nixon has always had a tremendous interest in Asia. "During the final third of the twentieth century," he said in 1967, "Asia, not Europe or Latin America, will pose the greatest danger of a confrontation which could es-

[50] *Nuclear Weapons and Foreign Policy*, p. 429.

[51] Richard M. Nixon, Address to American Legion, Los Angeles, September 6, 1956; *U.S. News and World Report* (September 14, 1956), pp. 107, 108.

[52] Richard M. Nixon, "Meeting the People of Asia," *Department of State Bulletin*, 30:12, January 4, 1954.

[53] Richard M. Nixon, "Facing the Facts in Vietnam," Speech to the Executives Club of New York, January 26, 1965. *Vital Speeches of the Day* (March 15, 1965), p. 338.

[54] Writing about Dulles in *Life Magazine* (June 8, 1959), Nixon said "History will record that the 'inflexibility' and 'brinkmanship' for which he was criticized in truth represented basic principles of the highest order."

calate into World War III."[55] The foundations of the Kissinger-Nixon Doctrine can be found, not only in Kissinger's books but also in Nixon's words on Asia in the fifties and sixties.

The Nixon view of U.S. Asian policy in his pre-presidential days can be summarized as follows:

1. *The United States is a Pacific power,* which means that the U.S. will maintain a powerful military position on the other side of the Pacific. He repeatedly refers to the U.S. as a Pacific power, sometimes as "the greatest Pacific power," pointing out the "grimly symbolic" fact that we have fought three Asian wars in a generation. While Europe has been withdrawing the "remnants of empire" in this area, "both our interests and our ideals propel us westward across the Pacific."[56]

2. *Our interests and ideals are threatened by China.* It is vital to keep the people and resources of Asia from falling to Red China which is making "an all-out effort to win this area."[57] China is the real enemy everywhere in Asia, including Vietnam: ". . . the confrontation in Vietnam is, in the final analysis, between the United States and Communist China."[58] The Chinese threat (since the Korean War) is primarily from "internal subversion" and revolution in other Asian countries, rather than from direct aggression.[59]

[55] "Asia after Viet Nam," p. 112.
[56] Ibid.
[57] "Meeting the People of Asia," p. 10.
[58] Speech to Executives Club of New York, p. 339.
[59] "Meeting the People of Asia," p. 13.

3. *China understands only the language of strength.* History proves that the leaders of totalitarian states "have the type of mentality which respects strength and strength alone."[60] If they are allowed to "gain from their aggression they will be encouraged to try it again . . . those who advocate the hard line in Peking . . . will have won the day . . . and we shall be confronted with other Vietnams in Asia. . . ."[61] Furthermore, containment is not enough. "Along with it, we need a positive policy of pressure and persuasion, of dynamic detoxification, a marshaling of Asian forces . . . to draw off the poison from the thoughts of Mao."[62]

4. *The war in Southeast Asia is a battle for all Asia.* This is the domino theory. If Indochina falls, Thailand is put in "an impossible position" and the same is true of Malaya . . . Indonesia . . . even Japan.[63] In the long run, the Pacific could become a "Red Sea."[64] In 1967, Nixon claimed that the U.S. presence in Vietnam

has provided tangible and highly visible proof that communism is not necessarily the wave of Asia's future. This was a vital factor in the turnaround of Indonesia. . . . Viet Nam has diverted Peking from such other potential targets as India, Thailand and Malaysia.[65]

[60] Speech to American Legion, p. 107.
[61] "Why Not Negotiate in Vietnam?" p. 51.
[62] "Asia after Viet Nam," p. 123.
[63] "Meeting the People of Asia," p. 12.
[64] Speech to the Executives Club of New York, p. 338.
[65] "Asia after Viet Nam," p. 111.

5. *Noncommunist Asian nations, with U.S. help, must fight other battles for Asia.* This marks the major development in Nixon's approach to Asia since the fifties: the increased military role of Asian countries, backed by U.S. power.

These regional arrangements, based on "the common danger from Communist China," would deal both with "traditional war, in which armies cross over national boundaries, and with the so-called 'wars of national liberation,' in which they burrow under national boundaries."[66] This was one of the principal messages of his 1967 *Foreign Affairs* article.

The other nations capable of exerting "creative counterpressure" under "protection" of the U.S. are those that have "discovered and applied the lessons of America's own economic success," namely, "a prime reliance on private enterprise" (and, by the way, a "receptivity to foreign investment.")[67] With most of them, the U.S. already has military ties, so it is just a question of putting the need for a regional alliance in "sufficiently compelling terms."[68]

"I am not arguing that the day is past when the United States would respond militarily to communist threats in the less stable parts of the world, or that a unilateral response to a unilateral request for help is out of the question," he said. "But other nations must recognize that the role of the United States as

66 Ibid., p. 114.
67 Ibid., p. 119.
68 Ibid., p. 116.

world policeman is likely to be limited in the future."[69] Nixon did not develop this general approach —the Asian application of Vietnamization—until the late sixties, but he recognized a special role for Japan much earlier.

6. *Japan has a special role to play.* In 1954, Nixon saw a danger of "losing" Japan. To keep it in the anticommunist camp, Nixon maintained it was necessary to make Southeast Asia safe for Japanese economic penetration:

If this whole part of Southeast Asia goes under Communist domination or Communist influence, Japan, who trades and must trade with this area in order to exist, must inevitably be oriented toward the Communist regime.[70]

By 1965, the danger had been replaced by an opportunity:

The biggest prize of all is, of course, Japan, a miracle of development and the greatest industrial power in Asia— the only country with the possible chance to counterbalance China once China develops its industrial might.[71]

And by 1967, Japan was seen as the cornerstone of the military containment of communism in Asia:

Japan is expected soon to rank as the world's third-strongest economic power, trailing only the United States and the Soviet Union. Along with this dramatic economic surge, Japan will surely want to play a greater role both diplomatically and militarily in maintaining the balance in Asia. . . .

[69] Ibid., p. 114.
[70] "Meeting the People of Asia," p. 12.
[71] Speech to the Executives Club of New York, p. 338.

This greater role will entail, among other things, a modification of the present terms of the Japanese Constitution, which specifically provides that "land, sea and air forces, as well as other war potential, will never be maintained." (Japan's 275,000 men presently under arms are called "Self-Defense Forces.") . . . Not to trust Japan today with its own armed forces . . . ill accords with the role Japan must play in helping secure the common safety of noncommunist Asia.[72]

Nixon recognized some *internal* problems in remilitarizing Japan, where "public opinion still lags behind official awareness of military needs."[73] He mentioned no external problems. If the regional alliances policy sounds much like the postwar containment of the Soviet Union, that is no accident. Nixon considered that a success which could be duplicated in Asia.[74] But there is another disturbing parallel: the restoration of Japanese military power as a counterbalance to China is reminiscent of the restoration of German military power as a counterbalance to the Soviet Union between the two wars, a policy which even Nixon might consider something less than a resounding success. Nor is Nixon much concerned with the reaction of other Asian nations who have not forgotten Japanese imperialism and the "Greater East Asia Co-Prosperity Sphere."

7. *Now is the time to deal with China.* As "now"

[72] "Asia after Viet Nam," pp. 120–121.
[73] Ibid., p. 116.
[74] Ibid., p. 124.

changed from the early fifties to the late sixties both the reasons and the tactics changed, but not the immediacy. At first, it was the "loss" of China by the Truman administration that required a new policy "now." By the mid-sixties, he was saying that "the Soviet Union and Red China are enemies not allies as they were at the time of the Korean War" and for this reason "this is the best time to stop Chinese aggression." Without its former ally, China is a "fourth rate military power," but time, he felt, was not on our side because in "Five years, ten years—we might not be able to make a stand there, or any place else without risking a nuclear war" while in fifteen or twenty-five years "Red China could become one of the great industrial powers of the world."[75] Meanwhile, it was safe to press for victory in Vietnam because China would not be likely to enter the war.

Nixon was still saying in 1967 that the world could not be safe until China changed, as he had been saying twenty years earlier, but he had long since given up hope of either internal collapse or overthrow by Chiang Kai-shek. In a passage remarkably revealing of his attitude both to China and to black people in U.S. cities, he said:

Dealing with Red China is something like trying to cope with the more explosive ghetto elements in our own country. In each case a potentially destructive force has to be curbed; in each case an outlaw element has to be

[75] Speech to Executives Club of New York, p. 339.

brought within the law; in each case dialogues have to be opened; in each case aggression has to be restrained while education proceeds; and, not least, in neither case can we afford to let those now self-exiled from society stay exiled forever.[76]

8. *The Vietnam War must be won, and it can be won if enough force is used. The end of the war should not be negotiated without victory.*

November 1953, speaking in Hanoi, then still in French hands, he said "It is impossible to lay down arms until victory is completely won." Repeatedly during the French-Indochina war, and again on this occasion, he urged the Vietnamese to remain within the French Union.[77] A year later, he said that if France stopped fighting in Indochina the United States would have to send troops.[78]

February 1962, dissenting from Republican criticism of Kennedy's steps to strengthen U.S. military assistance he said his only question was whether "it may be too little and too late."[79]

April 1964, he called for military strikes against communist bases in North Vietnam and Laos.[80]

January 1965, he proposed that the U.S. Navy and Air Force be used to cut communist supply lines to

[76] "Asia after Viet Nam," p. 123.

[77] *New York Times,* November 5, 1953.

[78] *New York Times,* April 17, 1954.

[79] *I. F. Stone's Bi-Weekly,* April 19, 1971. Stone devotes two of his four pages in this issue to Nixon's past pushes for deeper involvement.

[80] *New York Times,* April 17, 1964.

South Vietnam and destroy communist staging areas in North Vietnam and Laos.[81]

September 1965, he advocated an increase in American forces and a step-up in air and naval attacks on North Vietnam, specifically mentioning "military targets in the Hanoi area," and recommended consideration of a naval blockade of Haiphong. According to a *New York Times* story, "Mr. Nixon said he regarded the decision whether to retaliate directly on Communist China as contingent upon the depth of provocation."[82]

November 1965, he again pressed for intensification of the bombing, adding a recommendation for mining Haiphong harbor.[83]

August 1966, speaking in Saigon, he suggested that American ground troops be increased by about 25 percent. In a now familiar phrase, he justified this by saying that in the long run it would reduce American casualties. He continued to advocate intensified bombing of the North, and thought "a military justification" for bombing irrigation dikes in the Red River delta "might be arrived at."[84]

The danger of bringing China into the war was raised with Mr. Nixon from time to time in connection with these recommendations for escalation. His response was invariably that this was unlikely be-

[81] *New York Times,* January 27, 1965.
[82] *New York Times,* September 12, 1965.
[83] *New York Times,* November 21, 1965.
[84] *New York Times,* August 8, 1966.

cause "Without the logistical support of the Soviet Union, Communist China is a fourth-rate military power."

As President, Nixon has continued to repeat that the U.S. is a Pacific power.[85] He still finds China a major threat;[86] in spite of the recent thaw in Sino-U.S. relations, there is no evidence that the U.S. is prepared to reconsider any of the fundamental issues which have governed these relations for a quarter century. The Doctrine Nixon enunciated for Asia in July 1969 still threatens China with U.S. nuclear might, and the nuclear specter continues to hover over Peking even as Kissinger and Nixon negotiate with Chou En-lai. Nixon appears to be convinced today as he was fifteen years ago that the fight in Indochina is a battle for Asia, and that China holds the key to that struggle.

Economic and, even more, military aid to noncommunist countries in Asia, a perennial feature of U.S. foreign policy, is being stepped up by his administration, with considerable emphasis on police and paramilitary forces to control opposition to present U.S. client regimes.[87] Thus in 1970 the U.S. provided $150 million to modernize South Korea's military, $255 million for the Lon Nol government in Cambodia, mostly for the military, added $65 million to what had already been appropriated for South

[85] *Department of State Bulletin*, 64:377, March 22, 1971.

[86] *New York Times*, July 26, 1969, reporting on Nixon's Guam speech, which was not for direct quotation.

[87] 1970 "State of the World" message, *Department of State Bulletin*, 62:321, March 9, 1970.

Vietnam, and gave $30 million to Indonesia. Closely integrated with these Asian military forces are U.S air and naval power. Bases all around China's perimeter have stocks of nuclear weapons, and planes carrying nuclear bombs are regularly in the air in the Asian theater. Although U.S. ties to Chiang Kai-shek have weakened, U.S. military bases remain on Taiwan.

So far, the effort to build a pro-U.S., anti-China regional system in Southeast Asia has not been notably successful. Indeed, the administration's principal contribution to regionalism has been to transform the Vietnam War into the Indochina War—and in the process to increase the unity not only of the forces of resistance in Indochina but their ties with China as well.

The special role for a resurgent Japan has been implemented, however. The Sato-Nixon accord of November 1969 publicly endorsed Japanese claims that "the security of the Republic of Korea was essential to Japan's own security . . . (and) that the maintenance of peace and security in the Taiwan area was also a most important factor for the security of Japan."[88]

A quarter of a century ago, the U.S. imposed a peace constitution on a defeated Japan to insure that she would never again have the capacity to make aggressive war. Ironically, it is the U.S. which, for some years now, has been aiding and encouraging the outward looking military activities of Japan,

[88] *New York Times,* November 21, 1970.

though not, recently, without fleeting thoughts of a less harmonious era in U.S.-Japanese relations and a naval base called Pearl Harbor.

While Japan has yet to transform its nuclear capabilities into a nuclear arsenal, under the fourth defense buildup its military capability is slated to grow at an extraordinary rate. Parallel to the Nixon strategy of Vietnamization has been the effort to insure that a Japan still dependent on U.S. nuclear might and U.S. trade would assume increasing responsibilities for shoring up a shaky *Pax Americana* in Asia.

The war that Mr. Nixon "inherited" is the war he was eager to fight in the fifties; that he supported in the sixties; that he is not yet willing to end in the seventies.

Dr. Kissinger's Strategy for Fighting Mr. Nixon's War

Kissinger's reputation as a strategist was founded on *Nuclear Weapons and Foreign Policy* (1957) which attacked the Dulles strategy of deterrence based on massive nuclear retaliation. As Kissinger said in his preface:

Mankind has at its disposal the means to destroy itself at the precise moment when schisms among nations have never been deeper. And the attempt to come to grips with the horrors of the new technology confronts the additional handicap that we can draw only limited guidance from previous experience because much of it has been made irrelevant by the very enormity of modern means of mass destruction.[89]

But *Nuclear Weapons and Foreign Policy* addressed itself neither to closing the schisms among nations, nor to avoiding the use of nuclear weapons. Nor did it take exception to the basic goals of the Dulles foreign policy. It proposed making maximum use of nuclear weapons in a strategy that closely integrated diplomacy and force, while seeking to stop short of all-out nuclear war. Kissinger felt that no enemy would actually believe that massive nuclear retaliation would be used by the U.S. unless this nation's very survival were in imminent danger. If that were the only situation in which the U.S. would actually use massive retaliation, that would be the only situation it could deter, Kissinger said. What he advocated was a more credible deterrent, one which the U.S. would actually *use* where its interests, but not its survival, were at stake.

Kissinger's strategic doctrine called for the United States to maintain forces ranging all the way from small, mobile conventional forces up to the capability for waging all-out nuclear war, neglecting no level in between, so that graduated threats or uses of force appropriate to any situation could be employed. Limited war, what Kissinger called intermediate applications of power, may, he wrote, "bring much higher political returns than resort to all-out war,"

[89] *Nuclear Weapons and Foreign Policy,* p. xi.

and "offer the best chance to bring about strategic changes favorable to our side."[90]

Edging toward the Brink

A single paragraph in *Nuclear Weapons and Foreign Policy* clearly embodies Kissinger's view of the failure of the Dulles strategy and the rationale for limited war, simultaneously revealing that his strategy is only a different and perhaps even more dangerous kind of brinkmanship. This passage is also interesting because it indicates that in 1957, when the U.S. was not deeply involved in Indochina, Kissinger was apparently ready to "confront" the "risks" involved in seeking a military solution there.

The key problem of present-day strategy is to devise a spectrum of capabilities with which to resist Soviet challenges. These capabilities should enable us to confront the opponent with contingencies from which he can extricate himself *only* by all-out war, while deterring him from this step by a superior retaliatory capacity. Since the most difficult decision for a statesman is whether to risk the national substance by unleashing an all-out war, the psychological advantage will always be on the side of the power which can shift to its opponent the decision to initiate all-out war. All Soviet moves in the postwar period have had this character. They have faced us with problems which by themselves did not seem worth an all-out war, but with which we could not deal by an alternative capability. We refused to defeat the Chinese

90 Ibid., p. 147.

in Korea because we were unwilling to risk an all-out conflict. We saw no military solution to the Indochinese crisis without accepting risks which we were reluctant to confront. We recoiled before the suggestion of intervening in Hungary lest it unleash a thermonuclear holocaust. A strategy of limited war might reverse or at least arrest this trend. Limited war is thus not an alternative to massive retaliation, but its complement. It is the capability for massive retaliation which provides the sanction against expanding the war.[91]

The brinkmanship that insists on pressing a limited war to the point where the only alternatives before the enemy are defeat or unlimited war is revealed in another way in Kissinger's critique of U.S. strategy in the Korean War. He viewed U.S. intervention there as a "major act of statesmanship."[92] But he severely criticized its conduct, because it was *too limited*. While reading his comments on the Korean War, it is well to remember that Kissinger is now in a position to apply the same conceptions of risk-taking, and the same evaluation of worthy goals to the Indochina War, with immediate practical consequences for both Asian and American people.

He suggests that in Korea we should have "set ourselves more ambitious goals," although there were two risks: that the war would spread in Asia, but without becoming an all-out war, or that it would become an all-out war between the U.S. and the Soviet bloc. Nevertheless, we should have taken the chance:

[91] Ibid., pp. 144–145.
[92] *Necessity for Choice*, p. 1.

Had we pushed back the Chinese armies even to the narrow neck of the Korean peninsula, we would have administered a setback to Communist power in its first trial at arms with the free world. This might have caused China to question the value of its Soviet alliance while the USSR would have been confronted with the dilemma of whether it was "worth" an all-out war to prevent a limited defeat of its ally.[93]

To implement a strategy of limited war not only requires "a military capability which is truly graduated" but also "a diplomacy which can keep each conflict from being considered the prelude to a final showdown" although "we can make a strategy of limited war stick only if we leave no doubt about our readiness and our ability to face a final showdown."[94]

Kissinger gives some attention to how a war is to be kept limited. One kind of limited war which comes in for a great deal of discussion in his first book is war between major powers when there is a *tacit agreement* not to escalate. He even goes so far as to say that ". . . in a period of the most advanced technology, battles will approach the stylized contests of the feudal period which served as much as a test of will as a trial of strength."[95] While later books did not repeat such fantasies as this, in 1965 he was still advocating *early use of tactical nuclear weapons* in NATO European strategy, in the hope that a

[93] *Nuclear Weapons and Foreign Policy,* p. 49.
[94] Ibid., p. 173.
[95] Ibid., p. 226.

standstill in military operations could be forced and a war in that theater could remain limited:

There may be no *logical* stopping place once nuclear weapons are used. There is, however, a very crucial *psychological* obstacle to automatic escalation. When mutual invulnerability guarantees catastrophic destruction and offers no prospect of great military advantage, neither side can be very eager to let escalation proceed automatically. Both sides are likely to look for excuses to limit, not expand, military operations.[96]

A war in which both sides are "looking for excuses to limit military operations," is a strange war, indeed. In fact, the more one pursues the implications of the Kissinger limited war strategy, the more it becomes clear that it is not applicable to rather evenly matched enemies, but to a different situation: war which he describes as inherently limited because of disparity in power. In recent years, Kissinger has recognized that direct aggression by the USSR against Western Europe or the United States is unlikely, further emphasizing that intermediate applications of U.S. power are likely to be used against smaller or less industrially developed nations.

Even in his first book, he described this kind of war, giving as an example a war between the U.S. and Nicaragua, which would be all-out on the Nicaraguan side, but, whatever our objective, limited on the U.S. side, with the variation of a war in which the stronger power is "restrained from exerting its full potential

[96] *The Troubled Partnership, A Re-Appraisal of the Atlantic Alliance* (New York: McGraw-Hill, 1965), p. 181.

by moral, political or strategic considerations," as the U.S. was in Korea.[97]

The U.S. is now waging this kind of limited war in Indochina.

Starting a Limited War

There was so much talk in *Nuclear Weapons and Foreign Policy* about the opportunities presented by a limited war, that Kissinger's strategy seemed to include initiating such a war. This impression was strengthened when he raised the question of whether our strategic interest was limited only to opposing the forcible expansion of communism, or whether "the existence of a Communist regime in some areas" is "a threat to our security, however the regime is established. Do we resist Communist domination of an area only when it is 'illegal' or because the domination of Eurasia by communism would upset the strategic balance against us?"[98] he asked.

In his next book, *The Necessity for Choice*, Kissinger hastens to say that "No responsible person advocates *initiating* limited war. The problem of limited war will arise only in case of Communist aggression or blackmail."[99] His definition of communist aggression or blackmail, however, is extremely broad. At various times in his books, he includes in this category the events leading to our intervention in Korea and in Vietnam, the Soviet missiles in Cuba,

[97] *Nuclear Weapons and Foreign Policy*, p. 137.
[98] Ibid., p. 252.
[99] *Necessity for Choice*, p. 64.

China's action in Tibet and its border dispute with India, the Soviet supplying of arms to Egypt, the Soviet moves in Hungary and Czechoslovakia, the pressure on Berlin, communist influence in the Congo, and various other unspecified interventions by the USSR and China in third world countries.

The threat, *or use* of force—for Kissinger does not believe the U.S. should make threats it is not willing to carry through—may therefore be initiated in response to a wide spectrum of actions by other nations, even the legal election of a government unacceptable to the U.S. In spite of a somewhat less belligerent tone, his most recent book still advocates placing this country's alleged national interest above another country's legal right to choose its own government. "We find it hard to articulate a truly vital interest which we would defend however 'legal' the challenge,"[100] he complains. We may, as Kissinger says, find it difficult to articulate such a policy. Government spokesmen prefer to present a different image to their own people and to the world, but the U.S. has not hesitated to *act* on such a policy. The Pentagon study of the Vietnam War makes it clear that the U.S. government assumed it had a vital interest in forestalling the possible unification of the country under a communist, procommunist, or neutralist government, an interest which overrode the legal requirement of the Geneva Conference to hold unification elections. Similar action in another country

[100] *American Foreign Policy*, p. 92.

would be perfectly consistent with the Kissinger strategy.

Nuclear War against China?

The growth of the Soviet nuclear stockpile and the increased significance of long-range missiles forced Kissinger to reappraise his 1957 argument that limited nuclear war would be to the advantage of the U.S. and the disadvantage of the USSR. China, however, does not have such a stockpile. And that brings us to the heart of the contemporary crisis. All of Kissinger's original arguments for limited nuclear war against the Soviet Union now apply to China. Although China has conducted several successful nuclear tests and has recently launched satellites, U.S. nuclear superiority over China is probably far greater than it was over the Soviet Union in 1957. Furthermore, although Kissinger recognized the political disadvantage of using nuclear weapons against a nonnuclear power, he never completely ruled them out:

In a police action against a nonnuclear minor power, in a civil war in which the population must be won over, the use of nuclear weapons *may* be unnecessary or unwise for either political or psychological reasons. . . . The problem of limited nuclear war arises *primarily* in actions against nuclear powers *or against powers with vast resources of manpower* which are difficult to overcome with conventional technology.[101] (Emphasis added.)

[101] *Nuclear Weapons and Foreign Policy,* p. 189.

He has always seen the superior industrial and nuclear technology of the U.S. as a source of strength which compensates for the larger conventional forces of an opponent. That is one of his justifications for an important role for tactical nuclear weapons in Europe: For a nation like the U.S., he says, the "strategically most productive form of war is to utilize weapons of an intermediate range of destructiveness" meaning some of the smaller nuclear weapons, because these are "sufficiently destructive so that manpower cannot be substituted for technology" by the other side. In the same passage, he points out that the destructiveness of the individual weapons was "too small" in Korea, and therefore Communist China was able to substitute manpower for technology.[102]

The opening of a diplomatic channel to China (culminating in resumption of formal relations) fits in perfectly with the Kissinger view of international relations and with a determined effort to take advantage of the "difficult challenges and new opportunities" that have arisen from the Sino-Soviet split. Recall the Kissinger formula that force without diplomacy is "immoderate in triumph and panicky in adversity." As long as U.S. leaders were unable to talk to Chinese leaders, the U.S. was limited to force without diplomacy. Whether Kissinger would consider that the U.S. had at any time since World War II been immoderate in triumph in Asia, the situation in Indochina was beginning to present the danger

[102] Ibid., p. 194.

that we might become panicky in adversity. But the other half of his formula is that "diplomacy which is not related to a plausible employment of force is sterile."

Kissinger once wanted to confront the Soviet Union with the dilemma of whether it was worth an all-out war to prevent a limited defeat of its then-ally, China, a confrontation risking that all-out war. The parallel in the seventies would be to confront China with the dilemma of whether it is worth an all-out war to prevent a limited defeat of its ally, North Vietnam. Or, with China and the Soviet Union in conflict, *both* nations might be confronted with this dilemma, in the hope that they would not engage in joint or parallel action and that neither would risk all-out war to prevent a defeat of its Indochinese allies.

Nuclear Weapons Today

The Kissinger-Nixon Doctrine, as expressed in the 1971 "State of the World" message emphasizes a limited war strategy, with an important role for nuclear weapons:

—To deter conventional aggression, we and our allies together must be capable of posing unacceptable risks to potential enemies. We must not be in a position of being able to employ only strategic weapons to meet challenges to our interests. *On the other hand, having a full range of options does not mean that we will necessarily limit our response to the level or intensity chosen by an enemy.* Potential enemies must know that we will respond to whatever degree is required to protect our interests. They must also know that they will only worsen their situation by escalating the level of violence.[103] (Emphasis added.)

In regard to Europe:

Sole reliance on conventional forces might lead an aggressor to conclude that we might accept the loss of vital territory without taking further action. Sole reliance on nuclear forces, on the other hand, might lead inevitably and unnecessarily to the very widespread devastation that we should be trying to prevent. Neither of these prospects enhances our security.[104]

The Doctrine makes it clear that the U.S. can itself no longer substitute manpower for nuclear technology, and, by Kissinger's logic, this increases the likelihood of resort to small nuclear weapons of an "intermediate range of destructiveness."

Earl Ravenal, former Director of the Asian Division (Systems Analysis) in the Office of the Secretary of Defense, writing in *Foreign Affairs,* drew similar conclusions.

Essentially we are to support the same level of potential involvement with smaller conventional forces. The specter of intervention will remain, but the risk of defeat or stalemate will be greater; or the nuclear threshhold will be lower.[105]

An article on nuclear policy written about the same time by Robert Lawrence of the University of Arizona,

[103] *Department of State Bulletin,* 64:354, March 22, 1971.
[104] Ibid., p. 353.
[105] Earl Ravenal, "The Nixon Doctrine and Our Asian Commitments," *Foreign Affairs,* 49 (January 1971): 201.

former Defense Department consultant, discussed the opportunity rather than the danger presented by nuclear weapons, much in the Kissinger manner. It was published in the French *Revue Militaire Générale* but received widespread notice in this country because someone called it to the attention of C. L. Sulzberger of the *New York Times.* Sulzberger, basing his column of November 15, 1970, on Lawrence's article, wrote:

The greatest lesson of the Vietnam war is that America still has many commitments abroad and still retains foreign policy aims that can no longer be maintained by the kind of military establishment, strategy or network of alliances now employed. . . .

Limited commitments to conventional defense are seen as increasingly outmoded, yet total warfare is a dreadful absurdity. . . .

Consequently, the search focuses on a third solution. The answer may well lie in the field of truly tactical atomic weapons.

The suggestion is for the research and development of "purely fission warheads measured in tons" (rather than kilotons) and "neutron warheads." Although "This is not meant to include those devices now loosely called tactical, whose destructive power, although immensely smaller than that of the so-called strategic weapons, is often measured in kilotons," Sulzberger says:

The argument is that democratic societies can no longer limit themselves to weapons known to be outmoded but must find new arms whose power is not wholly unrestricted, *even to the extent of the so-called tactical A-bombs in today's arsenal.* (Emphasis added.)

Sulzberger quotes Lawrence to the effect that "Minor powers have shown an ability to frustrate U.S. conventional capabilities." One place a "minor power" has shown such an ability is in Vietnam. The implication of this argument is that nuclear weapons—even in the kiloton range, should be used in such situations.

Of course there is the old problem of public revulsion against the use of nuclear weapons that has bothered Kissinger since the fifties when he said that we required a "diplomacy which seeks to break down the atmosphere of special horror which now surrounds the use of nuclear weapons."[106] Kissinger objected to having the nuclear arm of the U.S. military tied behind its back by moral scruples. Addressing this same question, Sulzberger found an appropriate quotation from Bismarck:

We live in a wondrous time in which the strong is weak because of his moral scruples and the weak grows strong because of his audacity.

(Sulzberger does not give a source. The quotation can be found in *Die Politischen Reden des Fursten Bismarck, Historische-kritische Gesamtausgabe.*[107] It can also be found in "The White Revolutionary: Reflections on Bismarck" by Henry A. Kissinger.)[108]

[106] *Nuclear Weapons and Foreign Policy,* p. 190.
[107] Horst Kohl, ed. (Stuttgart, Germany, 1892), p. 110.
[108] "The White Revolutionary: Reflections on Bismarck," *Daedalus* (Summer 1968), p. 906.

The Doctrine Applied to Indochina

The Doctrine applies not only to Europe and to future situations that may arise in Asia. It applies very specifically to the limited war in which the U.S. is now involved. Here, too, Kissinger was prepared before coming to the White House with a plan for fighting a limited war that was part and parcel of his larger strategy.

The purpose of limited war, he says, "is to inflict losses or to pose risks for the enemy out of proportion to the objectives under dispute."[109] He explains that it should be fought by applying "graduated amounts of destruction" alternately with "breathing spaces for political contacts."[110]

Here is the heart of Kissinger's military strategy. While the destruction inflicted or threatened should be out of proportion to what the enemy will gain by continuing the war, during the breathing spaces diplomacy should offer a settlement sufficiently attractive to give him a reason for ending the fighting.

. . . limited war cannot be conceived as a small all-out war with a series of uninterrupted blows prepared in secrecy until the opponent's will is broken. On the contrary, it is important to develop a concept of military operations conducted in phases which permit an assessment of the risks and possibilities for settlement at each stage before recourse is had to the next phase of operations.

[109] *Nuclear Weapons and Foreign Policy*, p. 145.
[110] Ibid., pp. 156–157.

Paradoxical as it may seem in the jet age, strategic doctrine should address itself to the problem of slowing down, if not the pace of military operations, at least the rapidity with which they succeed each other. Strategic doctrine must never lose sight of the fact that its purpose is to affect the will of the enemy, not to destroy him, and that war can be limited only by presenting the enemy with an unfavorable calculus of risks.[111]

If, after one breathing space, the enemy does not evaluate "the calculus of risks" as unfavorable, the next round will hit him harder (graduated amount of force). The second round of diplomacy will offer another settlement. Kissinger always insists upon meeting *or exceeding* the enemy's force levels. If conventional forces are matched by the enemy, only nuclear force remains.

At no time prior to his appointment to his present post did he ever question the ability of the U.S. to exert all the necessary force. Even in 1960, when he said, "Fifteen years more of a deterioration of our position in the world such as we have experienced since World War II would find us reduced to Fortress America . . ."[112] he saw the U.S. as strong enough to resist the strategic transformations unfavorable to it, and to attain those that were favorable, once the proper doctrine and strategy were adopted. That is, Kissinger has always seen the U.S. as strong enough to persuade and coerce other nations until its desired objectives are imposed. He says emphatically that

[111] Ibid., pp. 225–226.
[112] *Necessity for Choice*, p. 1.

however much we rely on the conventional forces of our allies, "It would be risky to create the impression that we would acquiesce in a conventional defeat in vital areas."[113] The implication is that in Indochina, for example, if faced with a conventional defeat, we should seek a nuclear victory.

When Kissinger wrote about Vietnam negotiations shortly before coming to the White House, he believed it would be possible to bring the other side to accept U.S. terms because North Vietnam faced the alternatives of destruction or the loss of its autonomy to the USSR or China: ". . . we are so powerful that Hanoi is simply unable to defeat us,"[114] and "a continuation of the war will require a degree of foreign assistance which may threaten Hanoi's autonomy. This Hanoi has jealously guarded until now. A prolonged, even if ultimately victorious, war might leave Vietnam so exhausted as to jeopardize the purpose of decades of struggle."[115]

When the Nixon administration took office, Kissinger was in a position to begin utilizing his strategy of alternate "breathing spaces for diplomacy" and "graduated amounts of destruction" to impose U.S. terms.

Diplomacy #1

After months of haggling over the location of the peace talks and who should participate, the stage was

[113] Ibid., p. 91.
[114] *American Foreign Policy*, p. 129.
[115] Ibid., p. 128.

set for substantive discussions when the Nixon administration took office. Kissinger had played a role in establishing contacts with the North Vietnamese under Johnson[116] and there seems little doubt that he and Nixon were eager to utilize the Paris talks and other diplomatic channels to bring the war to a close. It was not clear to the public, however, what their terms for ending the war were, and what would happen if these terms were not accepted by the other side.

The peace offer made in Paris by Ambassador Henry Cabot Lodge five days after the Nixon administration took office demanded *mutual* withdrawal of U.S. military forces and of North Vietnamese "military and subversive" forces from South Vietnam, and "the right of the South Vietnamese people to determine their own future."[117] It is now abundantly clear that the latter phrase means keeping U.S. forces in Vietnam until the South Vietnamese government is strong enough to maintain itself in power.[118] In spite of minor modifications in the U.S. proposals, these two points have remained the basis of all subsequent peace offers.

[116] *Newsweek*, "The Kissinger Shop" (December 22, 1969).

[117] Department of State Bulletin, 60:124, February 10, 1969.

[118] In his speech before the American Society of Newspaper Editors, and in an interview with six newsmen, both in mid-April 1971, President Nixon stated that the United States would maintain forces in South Vietnam until the South Vietnamese have "the capacity to defend themselves against a Communist take-over," (*New York Times*, April 17, 1971) a capacity that South Vietnamese Vice President Nguyen Cao

Neither Kissinger nor Nixon was likely to make what Kissinger had called the "mistake" in Korea of stopping the fighting when starting the talking. Throughout the first months of the administration, the war in Vietnam raged on. General Abrams's orders were to keep up maximum pressure. However, there were certain restraints on the force that could be applied. The Johnson administration had stopped the bombing of North Vietnam in order to begin peace talks with North Vietnam and the Provisional Revolutionary Government of South Vietnam. Domestic opposition to the war had increased to the point where a long war with a larger American ground force was, as Kissinger recognized, politically unacceptable. The South Vietnamese army, despite U.S. efforts to strengthen it, was clearly unable to carry on alone —as the invasion of Laos would subsequently demonstrate. Other countries allied with the U.S. had only token forces in South Vietnam, and pleas for greater assistance in the past, for example by Clark Clifford during the Johnson administration, had met with

---

Ky estimated a few days later would take "15 or 20 more years." (*New York Times,* April 19, 1971). On April 4, Secretary of Defense Melvin R. Laird said that the United States would maintain a naval and air presence in Southeast Asia after American ground troops had been withdrawn from Indochina, a presence he said is required if the United States is to maintain a policy of "realistic deterrence" in Asia during the 1970s (*New York Times,* April 4, 1971). Asked about Laird's statement, Nixon pointed out that Vietnam itself is only "part of the reason" for our bases around Vietnam (*New York Times,* April 17, 1971).

little success.[119] If any U.S. troops were to be pulled out short of a peace agreement, some change in the other available forces would be necessary to prosecute the war. The administration announced a determined effort to make Vietnamization a reality.

All during 1969 the Nixon administration attempted in public and private talks to get the other side to accept its terms.

In the spring of 1969 the NLF offered a ten-point peace proposal which rejected the proposition that other Vietnamese were "foreign" or "external" forces in the same category as U.S. forces. It demanded a complete U.S. withdrawal and a provisional government "representing the various social strata and political tendencies" rather than leaving the present South Vietnamese government in control until elections could be held.[120]

The peace talks were deadlocked. But within a month after the first order for the withdrawal of U.S. ground troops (June 8) a drop in the level of combat was noted, suggesting that action by the U.S. toward withdrawal would be met with deescalation on the other side. On October 12, Secretary of State Rogers officially acknowledged that Nixon had changed the orders from "maximum pressure" to "protective reaction."[121] The level of ground combat continued to be lower throughout 1969.

[119] Clark Clifford, "A Viet Nam Reappraisal, The Personal History of One Man's View and How It Evolved," *Foreign Affairs* (July 1969).

[120] *New York Times,* May 8, 1969.

[121] *Department of State Bulletin,* 61:346, October 27, 1969.

Although summer brought a reduction in the ground fighting, it also brought the enunciation of the Doctrine for Asia, which showed the extent of the administration's commitment to victory in Vietnam and the extent of its commitment to Saigon. This made it unlikely that there would be any major change in the U.S. peace terms.

The Doctrine for Asia first stated by Nixon on Guam on July 26, 1969, threatened future Vietnams based on a combination of Asian foot soldiers and U.S. air power. But first the war in Indochina had to be won, or the U.S. position as an Asian power might be undermined. Although the Doctrine expresses caution about engaging U.S. ground forces against guerrillas, U.S. economic and military assistance, air and naval power, and if necessary, nuclear weapons, will be used to protect such governments as the military dictatorship of Thailand or the Royal Laotian Government. Without full implementation of the Doctrine to protect the Saigon regime, confidence in the U.S. might collapse elsewhere. Limited war might cease to be a "credible deterrent." As Nixon put it in an address to the nation on May 14, 1969:

. . . we have to demonstrate—*at the point at which confrontation is being tested*—that confrontation with the United States is costly and unrewarding.[122] (Emphasis added.)

[122] *Department of State Bulletin,* 60:458, June 2, 1969.

During the entire first year of the Nixon administration, with diplomacy being emphasized in administration statements and the first American troops coming home, many accepted the moderate appearance of the Doctrine, rather than probing for its hard core. But it was indeed being tested first and most sharply in Vietnam, and it is there that the Doctrine's aggressive dimension is being revealed.

Force #1

As the Nixon administration's first year approached an end, the diplomatic stalemate was publicly underlined. Ambassador Lodge resigned as head of the U.S. team at the Paris talks along with his second in command, leaving the third-level man, Philip Habib, as "acting head." Nixon indicated that he had no intention of naming a replacement for Lodge pending "a serious proposal" from the other side.[123]

In addresses in November and December 1969, Nixon deplored the diplomatic stalemate and threatened new military moves. He underlined this warning in a news conference at the end of January:

If at a time that we are attempting to deescalate the fighting in Vietnam, we find that they take advantage of our troop withdrawals to jeopardize the remainder of our forces by escalating the fighting, then we have the means —and I will be prepared to use those means strongly— to deal with that situation more strongly than we have dealt with it in the past.[124]

[123] Ibid., 61:619, December 29, 1969.
[124] *New York Times*, January 31, 1970.

According to Kissinger's guide to fighting a limited war, it was now time to graduate the amount of destruction upward. What means were available? Four moves had been advocated by various military and political figures (including Nixon) since the American build-up began in 1965: unrestricted bombing of the North, attacking and destroying communist sanctuaries in Cambodia and Laos, mining Haiphong harbor, and invading North Vietnam.

The ouster of Cambodian Prince Sihanouk in March 1970 provided the U.S. with a major opportunity for putting one of these proposals into action.

On April 20, 1970, Nixon made a major public speech in which he claimed that almost 40,000 communist troops were committing "overt aggression" against Cambodia,[125] while at the Paris talks, the U.S. spokesman was telling the NLF and DRV that their side's military activity was "not compatible with serious negotiations."[126]

On April 30, U.S. and South Vietnamese forces invaded Cambodia. A massive air attack on North Vietnam accompanied the invasion. U.S. troops remained in Cambodia two months, leaving a widened war behind when they withdrew.[127] This was in keeping

[125] *Department of State Bulletin,* 62:601, May 11, 1970.

[126] Ibid., 62:543, April 27, 1970.

[127] Secretary Rogers, in a press conference on February 15, 1971, admitted that U.S. supports South Vietnamese and Lon Nol forces in Cambodia by delivering weapons and supplies (this includes U.S. military equipment delivery teams), with U.S. air power used for logistics, for support of South Vietnam combat missions, and for independent bombing missions. *Department of State Bulletin,* 64:189–193, February 15, 1971.

with the Kissinger limited war strategy, a strategy that was explained by Nixon when he was asked how his escalation differed from Johnson's. Nixon indicated that Johnson escalated gradually, while he, himself, was changing the previous conduct of the war with a big, decisive move in Cambodia:

. . . the difference is that he did move step by step. This action is a decisive move; and this action also puts the enemy on warning that if it escalates while we are trying to deescalate, we will move decisively and not step by step.[128]

Diplomacy #2

Immediately after the withdrawal of U.S. ground troops from Cambodia at the end of June, the opening of the second diplomatic phase was signalled by the appointment of David Bruce to head the Paris talks, and by a statement from Nixon as to what he expected from this round of diplomacy:

You will generally find that negotiations occur, negotiations which end war, only when the balance of power changes significantly, only when one party or the other concludes that as a result of the shift in the military balance they no longer have an opportunity to accomplish their goal militarily and therefore they had best negotiate. . . . Cambodia . . . has changed the military balance.[129]

Yet Nixon's "decisive move," like so many earlier escalations of force, failed to achieve its objective.

[128] Ibid., 62:642, May 25, 1970.
[129] Ibid., 63:108, July 27, 1970.

Early in October, Nixon made a new peace offer, but without a substantial change in the previous U.S. position. Again, the other side failed to respond as Nixon thought it should. The diplomatic deadlock continued.

Keeping the Options Open

Domestic reaction to the Cambodian adventure made it clear that the use of U.S. ground troops in further escalations would be extremely unwise politically. However, the administration had been removing restraints on the use of air power, and resumption of heavy bombing in the North (as much as Johnson had ordered, or more) was now a possible option for the next graduation of force. Throughout this period, bombing of *Laos* intensified, and by June 1970 was reported to have reached 20,000 to 25,000 sorties a month.[130] Apparently, the bombing of North Vietnam never stopped altogether. In January 1969, the other side complained in Paris that the U.S. was bombing the North. Ambassador Lodge admitted only to action "to defend our reconnaissance planes and pilots when they have been fired upon."[131]

Secretary Rogers was still using the same rationale of defending planes and pilots when air attacks on North Vietnam by more than a hundred planes took

[130] Ibid., 63:83, June 29, 1970. (The number of sorties was mentioned in a question to Secretary Rogers at the Department of State foreign policy conference for editors and broadcasters in San Francisco and was not denied by the secretary.)

[131] Ibid., 60:145, February 17, 1969.

place simultaneously with the invasion of Cambodia.[132] Two months later, however, when asked about the possibility of a resumption of heavy bombing of North Vietnam, he replied, "I don't think it's appropriate for us to foreclose options."[133]

On November 22, 1970, U.S. planes bombed North Vietnam for twenty-eight hours. At the same time, the U.S. conducted an abortive raid on the Son Tay prisoner of war camp. The raid probably played a double role in American strategic design. It served as a warning to the North Vietnamese that their territory was subject to invasion, a message which would shortly be conveyed more explicitly. It was also the most dramatic step in the administration's manipulation of the prisoner of war issue to build domestic support.

In the very first plenary session of the peace talks in Paris, Ambassador Lodge said that "We seek the early release of prisoners of war."[134] In the months that followed, the Nixon administration made much of this issue and has tried to separate it from other issues being negotiated. However, the administration has made it clear that concern for the fate of the POWs will not be allowed to interfere with bombing the North, or any other requirement of U.S. strategy or tactics. As Frank Borman, Special Representative of the President on Prisoners of War said on September 22, 1970:

132 Ibid., 62:647, May 25, 1970.
133 Ibid., 63:85, July 20, 1970.
134 Ibid., 60:125, February 10, 1969.

. . . it is quite obvious to any student of the intercourse of nations that our course in Southeast Asia cannot be influenced in any significant manner by the treatment or the cause of the prisoners.[135]

Force #2

Action in Laos intensified in late 1970 and early 1971. In mid-December, the Pathet Lao reported stepped-up fighting in the Plain of Jarres. North Vietnam charged that more Thai troops were being sent to the Bolovens Plateau and to Long Cheng. B-52 raids along the Laos-North Vietnam border intensified.[136]

David K. Bruce said on February 5, 1971, at the Paris talks that the U.S. would carry out "alternative solutions to the conflict" unless serious peace negotiations were begun.[137]

Finally, Laos was invaded on February 8 by South Vietnamese forces with heavy U.S. air and logistical support. Again, as in Cambodia, the invasion was presented as limited in time and purpose. South Vietnamese forces withdrew by March 12, but U.S. bombing, which began before the invasion, continued afterward. The Laos invasion has generally been regarded as a failure. Certainly it was not a military success for the South Vietnamese forces who retreated in disarray with heavy losses nor did it bring the other side to accept U.S. terms for peace. However,

[135] Ibid., 63:405, October 12, 1970.
[136] *Bay Area Institute Newsletter* (Spring 1971), p. 6. Chronology from U.S. and French news sources.
[137] Ibid., p. 7.

it certainly increased the extent of the already great destruction in Laos and in the framework of the Kissinger strategy, that could serve as a warning of still greater destruction to come.

Diplomacy #3

In his elucidation of limited war, Kissinger emphasized the importance of developing "a concept of military operations conducted in phases which permit an assessment of the risks and possibilities for settlement at each stage before recourse is had to the next phase of operations."[138]

The third diplomatic phase could well have been used by the administration to assess its previous failure to evaluate properly the strength and determination of the Vietnamese and its failure to bring the war to a close on its own terms. But there were no signs of major changes in the U.S. negotiating position, in spite of strong sentiment in the Senate and the country for setting a date for total withdrawal, and a major peace offer from the Provisional Revolutionary Government of South Vietnam (the National Liberation Front) proposing simultaneous repatriation of U.S. prisoners of war and withdrawal of U.S. military forces.

The U.S. response to this offer, which effectively cut the ground out from under the administration's manipulation of the POW issue, was not to reject it outright but to bury the issue with a dazzling series

[138] *Nuclear Weapons and Foreign Policy*, pp. 225–226.

of diplomatic moves which replaced public preoccupation with the war with larger hopes for peace in Asia.

Henry Kissinger's China trip inaugurated a bold new phase in the diplomacy of the cold war, but there had been indications months earlier of this new phase in Sino-American relations. "At the time of the Laos invasion," Marquis Childs wrote in the St. Louis *Post-Dispatch* on June 1, "Henry A. Kissinger . . . stated without qualification his conviction that China would not send troops in to support the North Vietnamese. He based this, prior to the invitation to the American ping-pong team, on progress made through channels in establishing a new relationship with . . . China." U.S. negotiations with China are directed not only to insuring against Chinese intervention in Indochina in the event of another major escalation of the conflict, but to inducing Peking to pressure her Indochinese allies to accept peace terms acceptable to the U.S.

Nixon's overtures to China reflect an awareness at the highest levels of the administration of changing patterns of world power. China, Japan, and the Soviet Union all enjoy increasing strength in Asia, while the U.S. has been drained economically and divided politically by the Indochina War. Nixon's Kansas City speech of July 6, 1971, provides the clearest expression to date of his view of the new power balance in Asia. Nixon noted the rise of Western Europe, Japan, the USSR, and the People's Republic of China as major global centers of power *while the United States remained preoccupied with Vietnam.*[139] A month later the Nixon administration's dramatic attempt to shore up the sagging dollar and stimulate a stagnant economy with the most extreme economic and financial measures since the great depression provided eloquent testimony to the corrosion of U.S. economic power.

Economic and political troubles at home do not mean that Nixon has softened U.S. terms for victory in Indochina. Indeed, quite the reverse is possible. The failure to achieve victory via negotiations with China may precipitate a dangerous escalation of the Indochina War, including direct conflict with China. Behind the proffered hand of negotiation lies a nuclear fist.

The first diplomatic phase in 1969 created illusions at home that the war would soon be at an end. The Cambodian invasion dealt those illusions a hard blow, yet during the second breathing space new illusions were fostered, only to be submerged by the Laos invasion. During the third diplomatic phase, the approach to China again stimulated illusions that the end of the war was only a matter of time, in spite of the continued presence of U.S. troops and continued U.S. bombing. Illusions die hard.

Force #3

As the third diplomatic phase drew to a close, what further escalations were possible? A third blow

[139] *New York Times,* July 7, 1971.

would have to be more decisive than the Laotian fiasco. One possibility was a South Vietnamese invasion of North Vietnam with U.S. support. Since this had been hinted by Saigon leaders, Nixon was asked about it in his news conference of February 17, while the Laotian invasion was still in progress. The President refused to "speculate on what South Viet-Nam may decide to do with regard to a possible incursion into North Viet-Nam" but did not rule out American air support for such a venture. He said:

I am not going to place any limitation upon the use of airpower except, of course, to rule out a rather ridiculous suggestion that is made from time to time . . . that our airpower might include the use of tactical nuclear weapons.

The President listed some limitations on ground forces:

For example, we are not going to use ground forces in Laos. We are not going to use advisers in Laos with the South Vietnamese forces. We are not going to use ground forces in Cambodia or advisers in Cambodia . . . and we have no intention, of course, of using ground forces in North Vietnam. Those are limitations.[140]

It should be noted that the Son Tay raid on North Vietnam did not constitute what the administration means by "ground forces." The President's limitations as expressed here therefore do not rule out raids on North Vietnam by airborne or naval forces.

U.S. raids, unless on a big scale and accompanied by heavy bombing would be more symbolic than

[140] *Department of State Bulletin*, 64:281, March 8, 1971.

decisive. South Vietnamese forces numbering over 1,000,000, but with an effective fighting force of much less were already spread thin.[141] Nevertheless, "incursions" of one kind or another into North Vietnam were one possibility.

Another option was saturation bombing of North Vietnam. Many observers suggested this as the most likely move. Among these was Morton H. Halperin, who served as Deputy Assistant Secretary of Defense in the Johnson administration and on the National Security Council Senior Staff under Kissinger until his resignation in September 1969. Writing in the *New York Times*, November 7, 1970, Halperin said:

President Nixon's Vietnamization policy, far from getting us out of Vietnam, will at best lead to an indefinite presence in Vietnam of thousands of American troops. It could well drive the President to massive escalation, the mining of Haiphong Harbor and saturation bombing of North Vietnam.

Bombing of the North was tried by Johnson without success, but Daniel Ellsberg interpreted Nixon's view as that the Democrats moved too gradually and too predictably and had never threatened or used *heavy enough* bombing.[142] (Ellsberg is the former RAND Corporation analyst and former Special Assistant in the Department of Defense who has made the *Pentagon Papers* available to the public.) He suggested that Nixon's next "decisive" move might be

[141] *Bay Area Institute Newsletter* (Spring 1971), p. 2.
[142] Daniel Ellsberg, "Laos: What Nixon Is Up To," *New York Review of Books*, March 11, 1971.

. . . "decisive" bombing of targets long proposed by some U.S. military chiefs and their political spokesmen: Haiphong, "military targets" in Hanoi and unrestrictedly throughout the North, the dikes, the communications with China.

One of the most vocal advocates of this course in the past was Nixon himself.

The third available "conventional war" option was the mining of Haiphong harbor, although the ships of other nations, particularly the Soviet Union, may be destroyed. According to Clark Clifford, Johnson's Secretary of Defense, this danger restrained the Johnson administration from that step.[143] Rather than cutting down on the flow of Soviet supplies to North Vietnam, mining the harbor might bring heavier material assistance from the USSR, or even a stronger response.

None of these few remaining conventional options held the prospect of decisively shifting the war in favor of the U.S., yet all of them posed heavy risks. Heavy bombing of the North, especially north of the 19th parallel close to the Chinese border, carried the risk of bringing Chinese forces into the war, as happened in Korea, or of some other response from China. Ground invasion of North Vietnam, of course, greatly increases this risk.

The risk of bringing in China was there with the invasion of Cambodia but was "considered sufficiently remote so that looking at the situation on balance it

---

[143] Clifford, "A Viet Nam Reappraisal," p. 611.

was concluded that this was an acceptable risk."[144] The risk was greater with the invasion of Laos, which borders on China. The seriousness with which China looked at the Laos invasion was shown by the visit to Hanoi of a Chinese delegation headed by Premier Chou En-lai in March 1971 while the operation was still in progress. The joint communique issued by the Chinese and North Vietnamese at the conclusion of that visit also stressed the war in the air:

U.S. imperialism has now dispatched tens of thousands of U.S. troops and Saigon puppet troops to carry out a massive invasion of Laos in collusion with the Laotian rightist forces and Thai mercenaries. . . . What is more, the Nixon government has blatantly declared that it will not place any limitation upon the use of U.S. air power anywhere in Indochina. . . .

Should U.S. imperialism go down the road of expanding its war of aggression in Indochina, the Chinese people are determined to take all necessary measures, not flinching even from the greatest national sacrifices, to give all-out support and assistance to the Vietnamese and other Indochinese peoples for the thorough defeat of the U.S. agressors.[145]

Signals of peaceful intent have gone out to China prior to each of the Nixon escalations, but there have also been threats. Administration descriptions of the Doctrine emphasize that any action by China against a U.S. ally in Southeast Asia may bring the full military might of the U.S. into the conflict. The Doctrine

[144] *Department of State Bulletin,* 62:684, June 1, 1970.
[145] *Peking Review* (March 12, 1971), pp. 18–21.

states that if China enters the war all limitations on the use of U.S. ground troops and on the use of nuclear weapons are off.

In his 1970 "State of the World" message, and again in the 1971 message, Nixon said:

—the nuclear capability of our strategic and theater nuclear forces serves as a deterrent to full-scale Soviet attack on NATO Europe or Chinese attack on our Asian allies.[146]

And as Kissinger has said so often in the past, a deterrent which one is afraid to implement ceases to be a deterrent.

The article on nuclear weapons by Lawrence referred to previously, included a specific reference to China, and was quoted by Sulzberger as follows:

In the aftermath of Vietnam, we certainly do not propose to fight a large-scale conventional war with China. Yet the ability to engage Chinese military forces successfully may be a sine qua non of deterrence and stability in Asia.[147]

The implication is that "theater" nuclear weapons would be the way to engage Chinese forces successfully. Of course, neither Kissinger nor Nixon wants the threat of nuclear war to develop into its actuality. However, both the logic of the Kissinger strategy and the policies of the administration to date suggest conventional escalations that finally bring us to the very brink of nuclear war.

[146] *Department of State Bulletin,* 64:282, March 8, 1971.
[147] C. L. Sulzberger, *New York Times,* November 15, 1970.

During previous administrations there was always some hope that cool heads would prevail in a crisis, but one of the prime purposes of Kissinger's National Security Council system has been to prevent a veto on bold action. His criticism of former policy making claimed that it stressed "avoidance of risk rather than boldness of conception."[148] Cautionary advice from our European allies is also to be avoided.

Kissinger's entire system minimizes the opportunity for those who would avoid risk to affect the final outcome of a decision, with all national security affairs filtered through Kissinger, with the alternatives and their various opportunities and risks presented to the President by him. All the steps leading to a crisis may be taken, and finally the only alternatives may appear to be backing down or using nuclear weapons. When wise and humane counsel is needed, we may anticipate instead a confrontation called for by those "strong nerves" characteristic of the Kissinger ideal of statesmanship, that willingness to "face up to the risks of Armageddon"[149] in the hope that the other side will back down.

Kissinger has often told us that the use of nuclear power need not mean all-out war. Even if the other side does not back down, it is his theory that even nuclear war could remain limited, that only tactical nuclear weapons might be used. However, an article written when the use of tactical nuclear weapons

[148] *The Necessity for Choice*, p. 344.
[149] *Nuclear Weapons and Foreign Policy* p 173.

was last rumored to be under consideration to raise the siege of Khe Sahn in 1968 concluded that:

Tactical nuclear weapons introduce a new and vastly more destructive kind of warfare and are unsuitable for use if the civilian population is to survive.

A decision to utilize tactical weapons includes, at the least, destruction of people and property many times that of Hiroshima and, at the most, an all-out nuclear war with the possibility that whole *nations* may be destroyed.[150]

Whatever moves are made next in Indochina, they will grow out of the basic world view and strategic conceptions Kissinger and Nixon have evolved separately in the fifties and sixties and together since 1968.

As long as the war continues, the people of the world are faced with grave dangers. Kissinger's past record suggests that he will seek to advance the "legitimate interests" of the U.S. in Asia by relying on "the bargaining power inherent in our industrial potential and our nuclear superiority." But in the Kissinger lexicon, diplomacy never appears unless force is close behind. This means that should China or the Soviet Union interfere with those "legitimate" U.S. interests, war will threaten nations beyond Southeast Asia. An end to the war in Indochina, on the other hand, can open the door to new opportunities for peace in Asia and the world. Peace in Indochina is, therefore, more than ever the first item on the

150 Dan I. Bolef and Mark Antell, "Tactical Nuclear Weapons," *Scientist and Citizen* (now *Environment*) 10 (May, 1968): 91.

foreign policy agenda, as well as the first step toward returning to the American people a voice in their own destiny.

Epilogue: May 15, 1972

The third diplomatic phase has now been buried in the rubble of another round of escalations. The dramatic success of the NLF-North Vietnamese spring offensive, destroying in a single blow the façade of Vietnamization, presented the Nixon administration with the immediate choice of sharp escalation or genuine withdrawal. The U.S. unleashed not one, but a series of escalations in a desperate effort to turn the tide, intensifying the air war over North and South Vietnam, bombing Hanoi and Haiphong, and, finally, mining Haiphong harbor and bombing North Vietnam's rail links to China.

In confronting China and the Soviet Union simultaneously with the specter of war, Nixon clearly seeks to force them to accept (and pressure the Vietnamese to accept) a U.S. dictated settlement. But nuclear blackmail is not the entire story. Nixon is also offering the Soviets a major arms control measure and the Chinese the prospect of withdrawal of U.S. forces from Taiwan "as the tensions in the area diminish"[151] if they will permit the U.S. to pursue a military victory in Indochina. At this writing, it seems clear that both

[151] *New York Times,* February 28, 1972. U.S.-China Joint Communique at the conclusion of President Nixon's visit to China.

the USSR and China, though seeking to avoid a direct confrontation with the U.S., will stand by their Indochinese allies.

As the military situation in South Vietnam continues to deteriorate, continuation of the present U.S. course will bring the world ever closer to the brink of nuclear war. The U.S. has now exhausted all conventional options except the destruction of the Red River dikes and the invasion of North Vietnam. Only a reversal of the Kissinger-Nixon foreign policy can end the war in Indochina and put a stop to nuclear brinkmanship. Only statesmanship of a very high order in Moscow and Peking and strong pressure from the people of the United States can avert a holocaust.

II

GEOGRAPHY OF EMPIRE

KEITH BUCHANAN

RHETORIC AND REALITY IN EAST ASIA

Two decades ago, when U.S. Asian policy was described by political and military leaders and commentators in terms of the defense of freedom, democracy, and self-determination in Taiwan, South Korea, Indochina and other Asian nations, many Americans accepted this description at face value. Ironically, while U.S. spokesmen have bemoaned the "unpredictability" of China, their own policy pronouncements have ranged from advocacy of unremitting pressure on that country "in the hope that at some point there will be an internal breakdown" (Assistant Secretary of State Robertson, 1954) to claims that the U.S., rejected and rebuffed, has nevertheless "attempted to maintain a dialogue with the leaders of Communist China" (Secretary of State Rogers, April 21, 1969). The claim that China was "self-exiled" from the family of nations was made at the same time that the U.S. exerted its full influence to prevent China's entry into the United Nations and to pressure other countries from trading with her. When the People's Republic of China was described as expansionist, irrational, a threat to the peoples of Asia and to U.S. security, there was little dissent.

But the rhetoric has been wearing thin and the reality emerging more and more clearly as the nature of the "freedom and democracy" in South Vietnam has become obvious and as the basis of policy making in Southeast Asia has been revealed in the *Pentagon Papers.*

The reality of U.S. policy in East Asia can be seen in the pattern of U.S. military bases, combat forces and alliances surrounding China in a great arc from the southwest to the northeast. Beneath this arc, from Vietnam to Korea, many countries lie in the shadow of the U.S. military presence.

1. "Giving Human Dignity and Freedom a Helping Hand"
U.S. Combat Forces in East Asia, September 1969.

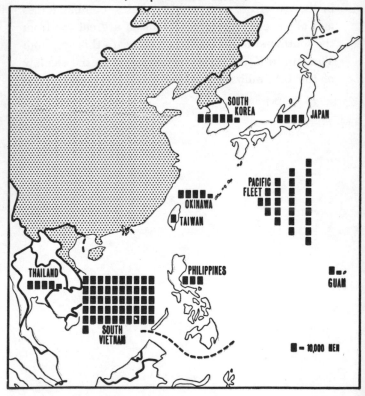

U.S. intervention in the third world is described in these words by U.S. counterinsurgency expert James Eliot Cross. Each black rectangle in this map represents 10,000 pairs of "helping hands"—a total U.S. combat force of approximately 1,000,000 men in 1969, reduced to about 700,000 in the summer of 1971.

2. The Real Bones of the American Military Posture toward Asia
Major U.S. Bases, 1969

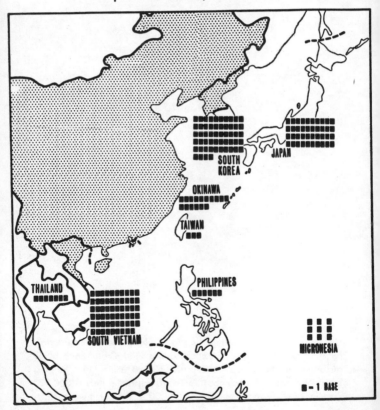

The determined resistance of the Vietnamese people, the de-moralization of U.S. and U.S. puppet forces, the growing world disapproval, economic crisis and deep divisions within American society have forced the U.S. government to reduce the number of U.S. troops whose role was, to quote former President John-son, "to help the good people of South Vietnam enrich the conditions of their life." U.S. forces in Vietnam were reduced below the 200,000 level by the end of 1971. But the real bones of the American military posture in Asia remain in the shape of a dense network of bases. These total almost 200 major bases and, as the map shows, almost half of these are only tenuously related to the Indochina conflict; the pattern acquires a logic only in relation to a policy of "containing" China and the Asian socialist bloc as a whole.

3. "We Are Not Seeking to Contain and Isolate China"
(Lines Indicate 1,000 miles Striking Range from Main Bases)

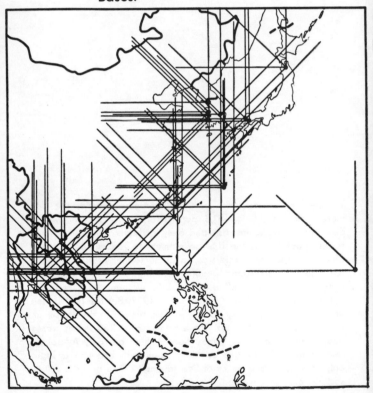

The reality as it must appear to most East Asians is suggested by this map, indicating the area within one thousand miles striking range of selected main air force bases. If this map is compared with a population map or an economic map of the region, it will be seen that the greater part of China's population and industrial potential is within less than one hour's flying time of major U.S. bases.

No part of the continental U.S. is within striking distance of existing Chinese aircraft.

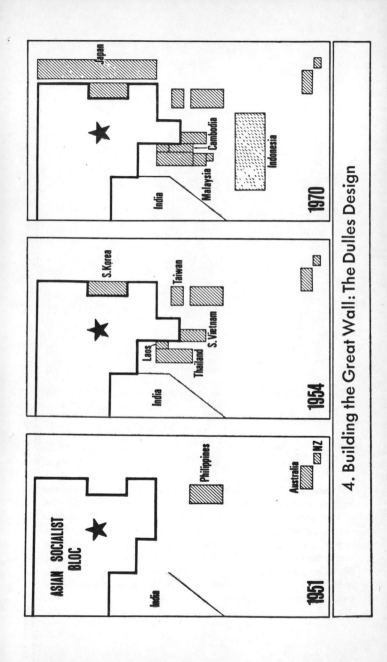

4. Building the Great Wall: The Dulles Design

From the Western Pacific bridgeheads represented by Australia, New Zealand, and the Philippines, the U.S. and its allies have step by step integrated the nonsocialist regimes of East Asia into an overlapping structure of military and paramilitary alliances. The point of departure was the Republic of the Philippines, with which the U.S. concluded a military agreement in 1947, and Australia and New Zealand, linked to the U.S. by the ANZUS treaty of 1951. A mutual defense treaty with South Korea legitimized the U.S. presence on the northeast margin of the Asian socialist bloc in 1953. SEATO (1954) drew in Thailand and linked Australia, New Zealand, and the Philippines, together with France, Britain, and Pakistan, in a policy of containment in Southeast Asia; Laos, South Vietnam, and Cambodia were included as "protocol states" (though Cambodia rejected SEATO protection). The U.S.-Japanese security pact of 1960 drew Japan into the pattern of alliances and ASPAC, ostensibly a nonmilitary but essentially an anticommunist grouping, drew Malaysia into a loose relationship with America's Asian allies. The integration of Indonesia into this U.S.-dominated design for Asia dates from Sukarno's fall and has been achieved by economic means. The Cambodian rejection was overcome when the Lon Nol government replaced Sihanouk and the U.S.-South Vietnamese forces dragged Cambodia into the "free world."

The Vietnamization of the World

The philosophy behind "Vietnamization"—the use of mercenaries and of the armies of client regimes in place of U.S. combat troops—has guided American national security planning for at least two decades. The increasing costs involved have, however, inspired a new emphasis on the financial, as well as the political and psychological advantages of employing "native" troops. Just as in the economic "development" of the "free world," the advanced nations, especially the U.S., supply the technology and the peoples of the third world provide the manpower and materials, so, too, in the military field, the U.S. provides the tools and the training and the local boys do the job, backed up by the helicopter gunships and B52s of the U.S. Air Force.

"Each partner," observes Melvin Laird, "does its share and contributes what it best can to the common effort. In the majority of cases," he adds, "this means indigenous manpower organized into properly equipped and well-trained armed forces with the help of material, training, technology and specialized skills furnished by the United States."

To insure the availability of this U.S. technological back-up, a dense network of army bases has been developed in key areas of the globe.

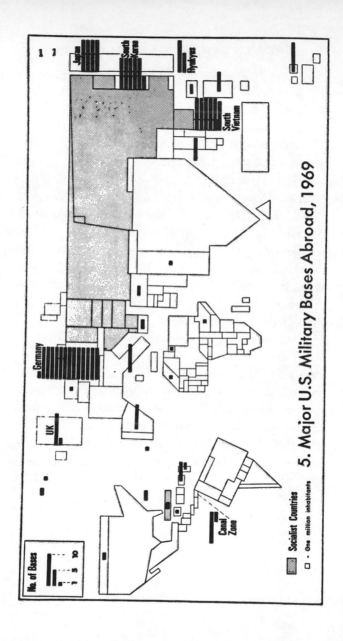

5. Major U.S. Military Bases Abroad, 1969

No. of Bases

1 5 10

Socialist Countries

□ - One million inhabitants

Germany

UK

Canal Zone

Japan

South Korea

Ryukyus

South Vietnam

Large areas of the European and Asian socialist blocs are within a few minutes striking distance of jets operating from U.S. bases. Adjoining seas are "protected" by U.S. bases (thousands of miles from the continental U.S.) and a dense pattern of army bases in Asia houses hundreds of thousands of troops.

The map emphasizes the overriding preoccupation of military planners with the Asian socialist bloc; here some ten territories contain almost one-half of the 399 major U.S. military installations abroad. And of the total of approximately one and a quarter million U.S. servicemen abroad two-thirds were, in late 1969, stationed in the Asian-Pacific region.

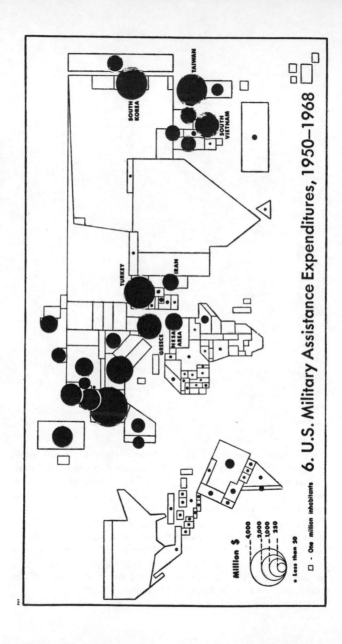

Million $

- 4,000
- 2,000
- 1,000
- 250

• - Less than 50

□ - One million inhabitants

6. U.S. Military Assistance Expenditures, 1950–1968

SOUTH KOREA

TAIWAN

SOUTH VIETNAM

TURKEY

IRAN

GREECE

NESA AREA

The Department of Defense figures on which this map is based show that $33 billion was spent over the eighteen year period 1950–1968, but this sum represents only a fraction of the total U.S. military assistance expenditures. It does not, for example, include military aid to South Vietnam since 1966 nor the inducements to South Korea and Thailand to supply mercenaries for the Indochina War (at least $1 billion in each case). Nor does it include the cost of a wide range of "support" programs. The figure would more than double if Agency for International Development (AID) funds were included. AID data for a period of only fourteen years (1953–1967) shows an expenditure of $62 billion, of which over $46 billion was for military aid and "supporting assistance" of a quasimilitary character.

Expenditure was approximately evenly divided between Europe and the Near East-Asian regions. But 95 percent of the aid to Europe was given before 1963, and of this almost one-third represented expenditures to enable France to fight the First Indochina War. Department of Defense figures thus indicate that the U.S. expended some $20 billion (three-fifths of all such expenditures) on military assistance programs designed to sustain her Mideast and Asian policies.

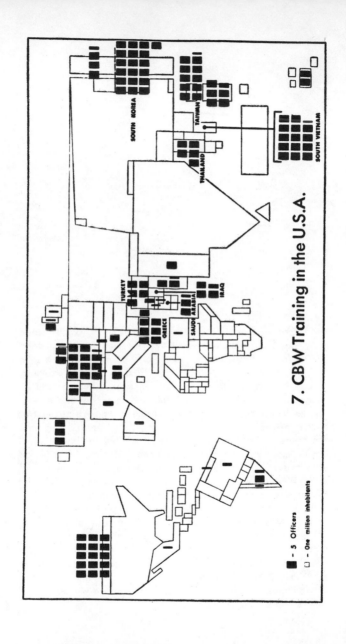

7. CBW Training in the U.S.A.

SOUTH KOREA

TAIWAN

THAILAND

SOUTH VIETNAM

TURKEY

GREECE

SAUDI ARABIA

IRAQ

■ - 5 Officers

□ - One million inhabitants

One of the more "specialized skills furnished by the United States" (to use Melvin Laird's felicitous phrase) is training in chemical and biological warfare (CBW). These programs—and the spatial pattern of countries taking advantage of them—give an extra dimension to the U.S. military plans for the third world. Against what enemies are the armies of Thailand, the Philippines, or South Korea developing their competence in this field? Note that CBW techniques are particularly suitable for use against the peasant populations of the third world whose malnutrition and low level of technology make them highly vulnerable. Moreover, unlike nuclear technology, CBW techniques can be readily mastered and weapons of mass destruction produced under relatively primitive conditions and at much lower cost.

To Have and to Hold:
The Economic Pattern of Empire

The Asian policies of the U.S. and its processes of global Vietnamization derive from an increasingly desperate attempt to maintain control over the greatest economic empire the world has ever seen. Says Claude Julien, of *Le Monde,* in *L'empire americain* (Paris, 1968):

The internal prosperity of the United States depends . . . in very large measure on her freedom of access to the natural resources of the entire globe, and more particularly those of the poor countries. The American economic empire, which in its reality is highly complex, is organized to safeguard and extend this freedom of access to the minerals and the agricultural products of the Third World, a condition which is essential to the maintenance of its internal prosperity.

The great gap which separates the U.S. from those nations of the third world which form the dependent territories of the American Empire is indicated by the table below:

National Income per Head 1968: Selected Nations

		$ U.S.	Annual growth percentage
Developed countries	United States	3,552	3.2
	Sweden	2,822	4.0
	Canada	2,250	2.8
Third world countries	India	71	1.3
	Ceylon	131	1.5
	Brazil	197	2.3

When U.S. consumption is measured against the finite character of our global resources, it is clear that it constitutes a major obstacle to the future progress of that two-thirds of humanity which dwells in the third world. Former World Bank President Eugene R. Black has said that if most of the people in the third world "are poor in the material things of life, there is in much of this area a wealth of resources waiting to be tapped." But if they are tapped by the U.S. economic empire, the gap between developed countries and the third world will continue to grow; the poverty of the many will deepen as the wealth of the few increases.

A growing proportion of this majority of humankind is beginning to understand that they are not backward and dependent because they are poor but that they are poor and backward because they are dependent and exploited. They reject the idea that they are "a resource to be tapped," and are beginning to move toward the idea that they themselves should tap their countries' resources—and for their own benefit.

8. Total Value of U.S. Direct Foreign Investments, 1969

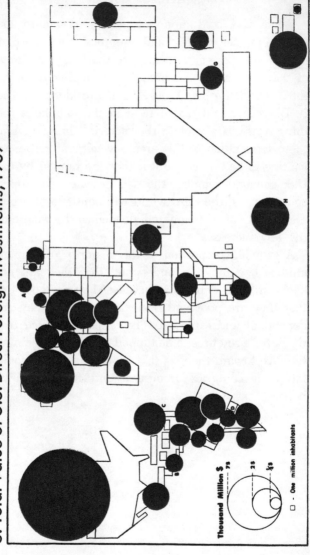

Thousand Million $

□ - One million inhabitants

The book value of U.S. foreign investments in 1968 was approximately $65 billion rising to $71 billion in 1969. Of this, approximately 30 percent was accounted for by Canada and a similar percentage by Western Europe. Twenty percent of all investments were in Latin America and only 2.5 percent in the Middle East; this 2.5 percent was, however, responsible for 14 percent of the earnings of U.S. investments.

Note to map: A: unallocated Western Europe. B: other Central America. C: other Western hemisphere. D: other Latin American Republics. E: other Africa. F: Middle East. G: other Asian/Pacific. H: International, unallocated.

9. Total Earnings of U.S. Direct Foreign Investments, 1969

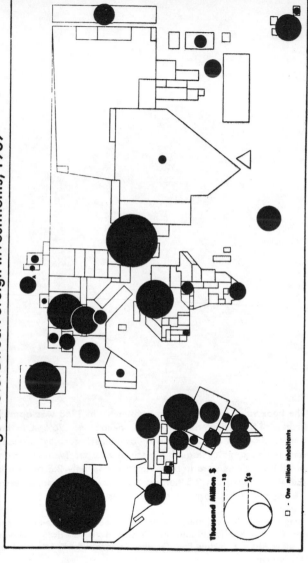

Thousand Million $

□ - One million inhabitants

The so-called less developed countries account for 28 percent of total U.S. investments overseas but account for almost one-half of the total earnings—and of the total earnings derived from these countries almost two-thirds is accounted for by the petroleum industry. The proportion of total overseas earnings accounted for by Canada and Western Europe is considerably below their share of U.S. overseas investments.

This pillage of the third world is an important element in what is, in simple terms, an updated version of the old triangular trade: very high profits on investments in the third world provide the funds which make possible an increasing economic colonization of the rest of the white north and of areas which at present are less profitable, such as parts of Africa and Oceania. Under these conditions, the whole system would be undermined if any sizeable sector of the third world should attempt to escape from the "free world" and begin to utilize its resources to improve the living levels of its own people. The Second Indochinese War and the pressures against the Chinese People's Republic were in part designed to demonstrate the retribution which such behavior would bring.

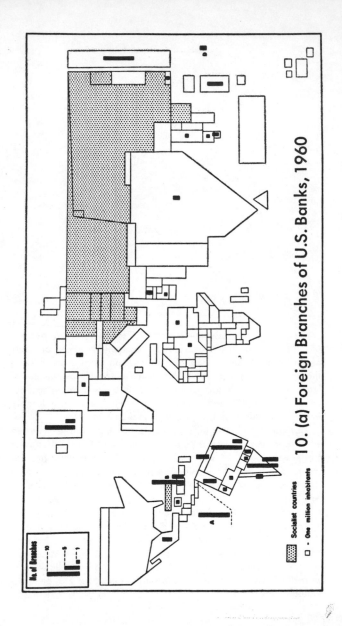

10. (a) Foreign Branches of U.S. Banks, 1960

No. of Branches
10
5
1

▨ Socialist countries

□ = One million inhabitants

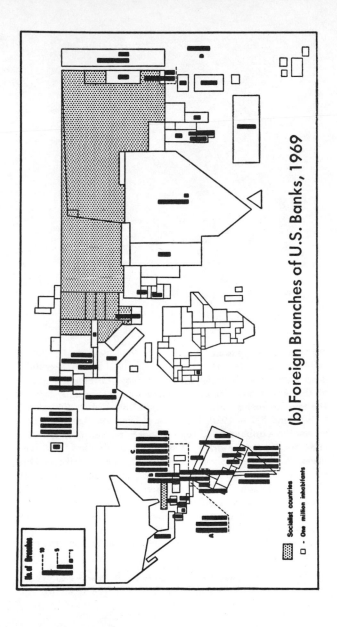

(b) Foreign Branches of U.S. Banks, 1969

The postwar expansion of the world activities of U.S. banks underlines the importance of finance capital in the imperialist process. In the last two decades the number of foreign branches of U.S. banks has increased fivefold and their assets, tenfold. The total number of branches has risen from 124 in 1960 to 460 in 1969 and 532 in 1970. The thrust of expansion has been, first, toward the Caribbean and Latin America, second, toward Britain and the Common Market countries. And, as the 1969 map shows, the bankers followed close on the heels of the military men and the politicians in Asia. The banker's role in the consolidation of Empire has been summed up by Rick Wolff: "The largest U.S. banks can influence the pace and the directions of economic development wherever they move. They exert such influence in the way they gather deposits, offer loans, affect local credit conditions and collect crucial intelligence on the local economy."

Note to map: A: Panama and Canal Zone B: Puerto Rico C: Bahamas and miscellaneous Caribbean D: Pacific Trust Territories

SOURCES

Rhetoric and Reality in East Asia

Data on U.S. bases and personnel is taken from *Global Defense: U.S. Military Commitments Abroad,* Congressional Quarterly Service (Washington, D.C.), September 1969. Data for Japanese economic expansion computed from *United Nations: Directions of Trade 1958–1962* and *1964–68.*

The Vietnamization of the World

Military assistance expenditures are given in *U.S. Military and Police Operations in the Third World* (North American Congress on Latin America). AID figures were taken from Richard Barnet, *Intervention and Revolution,* page 20. Details of CBW and CBR training programs will be found in *Congressional Record,* December 29, 1969, pp. 10992 sqq. *Congressional Record-Senate* for May 1, 1969 gives a listing of military-funded research projects and comment by Senator Fulbright pp. S4417 sqq.

To Have and to Hold
The Economic Pattern of Empire

Data on American investments and earnings is taken from the *Survey of Current Business,* October 1970. The *Annual Reports of the Board of Governors of the Federal Reserve System* give details of overseas branches of U.S. banks.

In the thirties economic rivalry between Japan and the U.S. for Asian markets became intense. By 1914 the Japanese empire had already expanded north north into the island of Sakhalin, east to encompass all of Korea, and south to take in Formosa and Okinawa. But in the thirties, Japan's imperialist expansion under the banner of the "Greater East Asian Co-Prosperity Sphere" threatened to engulf China and transform all of East Asia into a Japanese preserve, excluding the U.S. from a rich source of raw materials and a growing market.

Pushed back to her 1895 borders as a result of her defeat in World War II, Japan is now once more playing a major economic role throughout East Asia and beyond. Japanese economic growth, encouraged by the U.S. so that Japan could act as a counterpoise to the People's Republic of China, has now acquired a dynamism of its own.

South Korea, Indonesia, Taiwan, and the Philippines are shifting out of the U.S. orbit and into that of Japan. The maps which follow show the growth of Japanese trade only to 1968. In 1970, 40 percent of Philippine trade was with Japan. Japan also now accounts for five to ten percent of the imports of India, Ceylon, and seven of the smaller Latin American states, so the thrust of its economic expansion is not confined to the western margins of the Pacific.

Note, however, that owing to the penetration of foreign economies by U.S. capital some of the "competition" faced by U.S. industry undoubtedly originates not from "foreign" capital but from affiliates of U.S. industry established in the outer territories of the economic empire. A "Made in Japan" or "Made in Germany" label may be misleading in this day of multinational corporations, many of them U.S. controlled.

11. Japanese Expansion into the Western Pacific

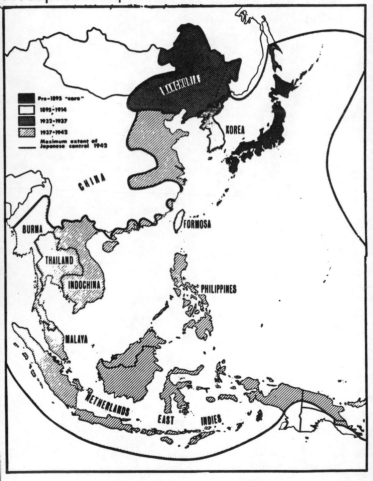

12. Japanese Commercial Penetration of the Pacific Region, 1958–1968

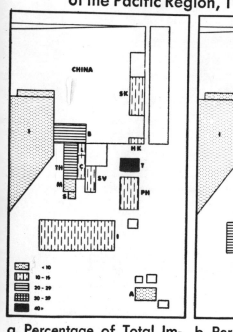

a. Percentage of Total Imports Supplied by Japan in 1958

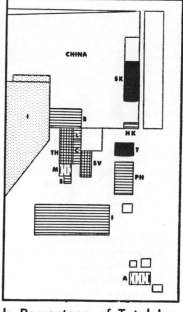

b. Percentage of Total Imports Supplied by Japan in 1968

Key territories in this expansion were Korea and Taiwan, and they have played a similar role in the process of U.S. expansion in the region since the Second World War. Contemporary Japanese economic expansion into the region follows the broad lines of her earlier military expansion, though the U.S. alliance has limited commercial contacts with China. The southward economic thrust of Japan, meeting the westward thrust of the U.S., is leading to an increasing clash between the two powers as Japan outgrows the role in which she was cast by U.S. policy makers.

These maps illustrate the broad front on which Japanese penetration of the region is advancing. In 1958 only Taiwan derived over one-quarter of its imports from Japan; a decade later, South Korea (42 percent), Thailand (37 percent), South Vietnam, and the Philippines had joined Taiwan. In addition, in 1968 Japanese goods represented over one-fifth of the imports of Indonesia, the Philippines, Singapore, Hong Kong, Laos, and Cambodia and slightly under one-fifth the imports of Malaysia. And the beginning of Japanese penetration of the South Pacific is indicated by the fact that 13 percent of Fiji's imports and 11 percent of Australia's imports came from Japan.

Though Japan is integrated with the Anglo-Saxon nations in the Pacific Basin Council, the dynamism of Japanese economic expansion is unlikely to be contained within such a grouping; rather do existing trends suggest the peaceful achievement of the Co-Prosperity Sphere Japan fought to achieve a generation ago, with the integration of the primary-producing Western Pacific countries into a globe-spanning economic empire dominated by Japanese finance and industry.

Rising Sun in Asia

The data for the diagrams of trade polarization is calculated from *United Nations: Directions of Trade.*

III

ASIA

AND THE NIXON DOCTRINE: THE NEW FACE OF EMPIRE[1]

JOHN W. DOWER

The Nixon administration's first statement of a new policy in Asia came when the President announced the "Nixon Doctrine" informally on Guam in July

[1] The present article has undergone several metamorphoses. The general analytical structure was first prepared in the fall of 1970 and appeared anonymously as Chapter 32 in Committee of Concerned Asian Scholars, ed., *The Indochina Story* (New York: Bantam, 1970, and Pantheon, 1971). This initial draft was also the basis for a presentation delivered at a conference dealing with American policy in the Pacific sponsored by the Institute for Policy Studies in Washington in September 1970; the contributions to that conference have been edited by Earl C. Ravenal in *Peace with China? U.S. Decisions for Asia* (New York: Liveright, 1971). A second and greatly expanded version of "Asia and the Nixon Doctrine" was published in the *Bulletin of Concerned Asian Scholars*, Vol. II, No. 4 (Fall 1970). Since then new information has come to light: in the *Pentagon Papers*, President Nixon's second "State of the World" address, Secretary Laird's "Defense Report" of March 1971, and a variety of other sources dealing with current American policies. More importantly, the Nixon-Kissinger actions toward Peking have forced re-evaluation of some of the basic assumptions initially used in interpreting the Nixon Doctrine. The present essay attempts to take these new developments fully into account, and thus represents a considerable expansion and revision of the earlier *Bulletin* article.

1969, but the precise meaning of that Doctrine has emerged only gradually. Existing transcripts of the initial briefing have never been published and cannot be quoted directly. Official discussions of the Doctrine, notably in the President's two "State of the World" addresses of 1970 and 1971 and Secretary Laird's "Defense Reports" of the same years, tend to be couched in general and ambiguous language. As administration supporters explain it, such ambiguity is deliberate and essential; any greater spelling out of American intentions would prevent the United States from being able to practice flexible and responsive diplomacy in the future. Or, even more subtly, the Doctrine is described as initiating a new era of dialogue between the United States and the world, and thus America cannot presume to explain it alone: "To attempt to define the new diplomacy completely by ourselves would repeat the now presumptuous instinct of the previous era and violate the very spirit of our new approach."[2] To critics, on the other hand, the Doctrine is little more than a political accordian; the administration's traveling minstrels, playing by ear, stretch it out or squeeze it tight depending on their particular audience. Invasion of Cambodia? *Rapprochement* with China? The Nixon Doctrine in action.

Despite this ambiguity, the general parameters of

[2] Richard Nixon, *U.S. Foreign Policy for the 1970s: Building for Peace* (Washington, D.C.: Government Printing Office, 1971), p. 20. This is the President's report to Congress of February 25, 1971, popularly known as the second State of the World address.

the Doctrine seem fairly clear. First, it projects the partial "disengagement" of American military personnel from Asia in the near future. This includes not only troop withdrawals from Vietnam, but from other countries as well. By mid-1970, in fact, troop withdrawals had been announced for South Korea (20,-000), Japan (12,000), Thailand (16,000), Okinawa (5,000), and the Philippines (9,000).[3] The essential ingredient in the new "low posture" or "low profile," in short, is that the most visible American presence in Asia—almost a million U.S. military personnel when Mr. Nixon assumed office—will be partially reduced.

The reverse side of this disengagement is Asian self-help. In the President's phrase, "Asian hands must shape the Asian future." Pro-American regimes are to be strengthened so that in the suppression of future "insurgencies" they can shoulder a major part of the burden borne up to now by the United States, notably in the Korea and Indochina wars. "Asianization," however, will still be closely integrated with American material aid, American tactical and strategic concepts, American air and sea support, and, in the final recourse, the American nuclear arsenal. This is the import of the President's often-quoted statement:

First, the United States will keep all of its treaty commitments.

Second, we shall provide a shield if a nuclear power

[3] Ibid., p. 18.

threatens the freedom of a nation allied with us, or of a nation whose survival we consider vital to our security.

Third, in cases involving other types of aggression we shall furnish military and economic assistance when requested in accordance with our treaty commitments. But we shall look to the nation directly threatened to assume the primary responsibility of providing the manpower for its defense.[4]

As recent examples of Asian self-help, the administration points to developments such as assumption of sole responsibility for patrol duties along the thirty-eighth parallel by South Korean forces; replacement of American personnel by Japanese in various military tasks in Japan and Okinawa; South Vietnamese military activities in neighboring Cambodia and Laos; and of course the "Vietnamization" program. Integral to the self-help concept is American encouragement of more explicit and self-reliant military alliances against projected "communist" threats in Asia: "The defense and progress of other countries must be first their responsibility and second, a regional responsibility." This projected regional defense network is described as being primarily a deterrent against China, and it is implicitly acknowledged that such collective alignments are not necessarily looked upon with favor by the countries

[4] Made in the first State of the World address, February 18, 1970 (*U.S. Foreign Policy for the 1970s: A New Strategy for Peace* [Washington, D.C.: Government Printing Office, 1970]) and repeated in the second. Unless otherwise noted, quotations from President Nixon are taken from these two addresses.

who are now being encouraged to form them. Defense Secretary Melvin Laird, for example, notes that "deep historical, social and political inhibitions to immediate effective regional mutual security arrangements in some areas must be recognized."[5]

The Nixon Doctrine is fundamentally a cost-conscious policy, aimed at maintaining a major U.S. role in Asia at less cost in both dollars and American lives. This combination has given the policy a racist cast perhaps best illustrated by Ambassador Ellsworth Bunker's comment that Vietnamization simply means changing "the color of the corpses." Former Defense Secretary Clark Clifford informed Congress in January 1969 that "an Asian soldier costs about $\frac{1}{15}$ as much as his American counterpart."[6] The present Secretary of Defense has synthesized this focus upon money and American casualties by summarizing the Nixon Doctrine as a blend of withdrawal-plus-Vietnamization. Laird argues that attainment of American objectives in Asia will depend greatly upon the effectiveness of the U.S. Military Assistance Program (MAP), which embraces military grants, training,

[5] Testimony before the House Armed Services Committee on March 9, 1971, p. 2331. Published separately under the title of *Defense Report*. The entire hearings are published in two huge volumes: Committee on Armed Services, House of Representatives, 92d Congress, 1st Sessions, *Hearings on Military Posture*, cited hereafter as *Hearings*.

[6] January 15, 1969, cited in Michael Klare, "The Great South Asian War," *The Nation*, March 9, 1970. The remark by Ambassador Bunker was reported in the January 15, 1970, weekly edition of *Le Figaro* and singled out by I. F. Stone in his newsletter of February 9, 1970; Stone describes *Le Figaro* as "conservative and pro-American."

weapons, and "specialized military support." In his words:

The Military Assistance Program is the key to this approach. It is the essential ingredient of our policy if we are to honor our obligations, support our allies, and yet reduce the likelihood of having to commit American ground combat units. When looked at in these terms, a MAP dollar is of far greater value than a dollar spent directly on U.S. forces.[7]

Thus, while the Nixon administration is economizing through manpower reductions and concomitant expenses in Asia, annual military aid and subsidized arms traffic is already greater than the average during the Johnson years. Under Johnson, less than $5 billion in annual military aid was officialy acknowledged. Under Nixon, corresponding figures have increased to $6.8 billion in fiscal 1971 and an estimated $7 billion-plus by the end of fiscal 1972.[8]

While the primary thrust of the Doctrine is military and budgetary, this thrust interlocks with important considerations concerning the future economic development of Asia. Here the President stresses interregional cooperation—"Asian initiatives in an Asian framework"—abetted by "multinational" corporations and organizations. At the same time, however, he acknowledges that in economic as well as military matters, "Japan's partnership with us will

[7] *Defense Industry Bulletin,* April 1970, p. 23.
[8] Earl C. Ravenal, "The Political-Military Gap," *Foreign Policy,* No. 3 (Summer 1971), p. 32.

be a key to the success of the Nixon Doctrine in Asia." The role of Japan is unquestionably of pivotal importance to the unfolding of the Nixon-Kissinger policy; it also represents one of the more enigmatic and unpredictable dimensions of the Nixon Doctrine.

The metaphor of the "low profile" has generally proven effective from a public relations point of view. The image projected is that of the wise man —balanced in outlook, powerful, yet restrained. This alleged new look, moreover, has already been dramatically applied to a core issue of U.S.-Asian relations: China. Mr. Kissinger's secret visit to Peking in July 1971 has forced even the most cynical Nixon watchers to acknowledge a dimension of imagination and flexibility previously foreign to the President's image. For many there is hope in the air. But the dynamics of American policy in Asia since World War II, and concrete though less flamboyant developments taking place within American ruling circles, suggest that at the very least this hope must remain suspended. Indeed, closer analysis provides many reasons for fear that, for the peoples of Asia, the Nixon Doctrine may prove to be more hoax than hope.

The essay which follows argues that despite undeniable policy changes, the Nixon Doctrine represents little more than the new face of American empire. It applies cosmetics to the scarred strategies of the past; here and there, where the old features of the imperium have become particularly battered, there is even a bit of strategic plastic surgery. At this stage in history, however, after two and a half decades of often tragic American policy in Asia, one looks for new questions, sensibilities, and commitments which strike to the root of affairs. The Nixon Doctrine fails to offer these. Upon close examination, it is fundamentally not even a new policy, but rather a pastiche of rhetoric and programs familiar since the early years of the cold war (section I). Despite the new China policy, containment remains the framework of military strategy; and despite impressive accomplishments by revolutionary Asian regimes, the U.S. has reaffirmed its commitment to counterrevolution (II). The network of American bases and manpower commitments abroad is being rationalized and restructured, not reconsidered (III). Client armies are being developed to replace American combat troops in crusades largely defined by Washington and at costs to both Asia and the U.S. which are as yet incalculable (IV). "Disengaged" American ground forces will be more than compensated for by major advances in military technology designed to permit new forms of intervention in the future (V). The possibility of the United States initiating nuclear war in Asia has been immeasurably increased (VI). Economic policies remain structured in such a way that many Asian countries face the prospect of becoming locked into permanent dependency as the neocolonies of either the United States or Japan, deprived of true independence or sovereignty (VII). Deep schisms within many of Asia's societies continue to be exacerbated by the imposition of America's preponderant power, denying those countries the possibility of self-determination. And despite appealing rhetoric of mutlipolar harmony in Asia, the Nixon administration has, in fact, generated new tensions in this area—a fact most strikingly obvious now in the U.S.-Japan relationship but extending far beyond this (VIII). These, in brief, are some of the conclusions developed in the pages which follow.

I

The Nixon Doctrine is not new. Like many of the President's views, it can be traced back to the consolidation of an American cold war strategy for Asia in the late 1940s and early 1950s. Parallels between American pronouncements during the military "disengagement" from the Korean War (when Nixon was vice president) and those now advanced in connection with "disengagement" from Indochina are particularly striking. For example, it was Eisenhower who, in early 1950s, articulated what is now a keynote of the Nixon Doctrine: "If there must be a war there in Asia let it be Asians against Asians."[9] Already futilely pursued by the French in Vietnam, the goal of training Asians to fight Asians was elevated to high policy under Eisenhower's Secretary of State, John Foster Dulles. Then as now, the prototype was "Vietnamization." A military training pro-

[9] Cited in James A. Donovan, *Militarism, USA* (New York: Scribners, 1970), p. 22.

gram for Vietnam, Dulles informed the Secretary of Defense in 1954, as the U.S. prepared to take over the French war in Indochina, would be "one of the most efficient means of enabling the Vietnamese Government to become strong."[10] The web of military pacts negotiated by Dulles—with Japan, Australia, New Zealand, and the Philippines in 1951–52; South Korea in 1953; SEATO in 1954; Taiwan in 1955—was not intended to be static. It was openly based upon the expectation of a gradual reduction of American troop strength in Asia as the pro-American regimes, particularly Japan, themselves developed larger military capabilities. Policy projections during the period of the Korean negotiations were framed in terms ironically close to those now offered the Vietnam War generation: American avoidance of future land wars in Asia; reliance instead upon American air and sea power, backed up by the nuclear deterrent; Asian self-help with American material aid and guidance; acknowledgment of the social and economic roots of the Asian dilemma and a verbal commitment to a more sophisticated, less military approach ("nation building"); cost-conscious slogans (the "economical" thermonuclear bombs, first tested in 1952, promised a bigger-bang-for-a-buck); and so on.

Consider, for example, the Nixon Doctrine against the secret National Security Council (NSC) policy statement of early 1952, which was released among

[10] The New York Times, ed., *The Pentagon Papers* (Bantam, 1971), p. 15.

the *Pentagon Papers*.[11] The Nixon Doctrine promises that through American military aid, "Vietnamization" will eventually permit total American withdrawal from Vietnam. The policy two decades ago was to:

Assist in developing indigenous armed forces [in Indochina] which will eventually be capable of maintaining internal security without assistance from French units.

The Nixon Doctrine bases its new "one and a half" war strategy to a large extent upon the conclusion that the stability of America's Asian allies is threatened not so much by overt Chinese aggression as by internal unrest: in the President's words of February 25, 1971, "The most prevalent Communist threats now are not massive military invasions, but a more subtle mix of military, psychological, and political pressures." But this "new" evaluation was also accepted by the NSC in 1952, as the U.S. began to deepen its fatal commitment:

The danger of an overt military attack against Southeast Asia is inherent in the existence of a hostile and aggressive Communist China, but such an attack is less probable than continued communist efforts to achieve domination through subversion.

Supporters of the Nixon Doctrine allege that much of its originality lies in the new emphasis upon regional responsibilities in defense. This, however, was also the course of action stressed by the National Security Council twenty years ago:

[11] Ibid., pp. 27–32.

Take measures to promote the coordinated defense of the area, and encourage and support the spirit of resistance among the peoples of Southeast Asia to Chinese Communist aggression and to the encroachments of local communists.

The Nixon Doctrine stresses a new era of economic regionalism plus integration of the economies of the underdeveloped areas with those of the capitalist world. So too in 1952 the goal was to:

Encourage the countries of Southeast Asia to restore and expand their commerce with each other and with the rest of the free world, and stimulate the flow of the raw material resources of the area to the free world.

The goal of Asian economic and cultural "regionalism" covertly guided into military channels by Washington was articulated even more clearly in the period immediately prior to the French defeat at Dienbienphu. Here are excerpts from the "Report by Special Committee on the Threat of Communism" submitted in early 1954:[12]

It should be U.S. policy to develop within the UN Charter a Far Eastern regional arrangement subscribed and underwritten by the major European powers with interests in the Pacific.

a. Full accomplishment of such an arrangement can only be developed in the long term and should therefore be preceded by the development, through indigenous sources, of regional economic and cultural agreements between the several Southeast Asian countries and later

[12] Ibid., pp. 35–38.

with Japan. Such arrangements might take a form similar to that of OEEC in Europe. . . .

b. Upon the basis of such agreements, the U.S. should actively but unobtrusively seek their expansion into mutual defense agreements and should for this purpose be prepared to underwrite such agreements with military and economic aid. . . .

Or, again, consider the following statement as a possible earlier draft of the Nixon Doctrine:

American combat troop involvement is not only not required [in Southeast Asia], it is not desirable. Possibly Americans fail to appreciate fully the subtlety that recently-colonial peoples would not look with favor upon governments which invited or accepted the return this soon of Western troops. . . . Any help—economic as well as military—we give less developed nations to secure and maintain their freedom must be a part of a mutual effort. These nations cannot be saved by United States help alone. To the extent the Southeast Asian nations are prepared to take the necessary measures to make our aid effective, we can be—and must be—unstinting in our assistance. . . .

The most important thing is imaginative, creative, American management of our military aid program. . . .

What we do in Southeast Asia should be part of a rational program to meet the threat we face in the region as a whole. It should include a clear-cut pattern of specific contributions to be expected by each partner according to his ability and resources. . . .

These paragraphs are excerpts from Vice President Lyndon Johnson's secret memorandum to President

Kennedy on May 23, 1961, following his tour of Asian countries.[13]

Fuller perspective on the Nixon Doctrine can be gained by noting in brief detail the history of two chief concepts: aid-plus-self-help and the anticipated role of Japan. It should be kept in mind, where aid is concerned, that no postwar American administration has ever claimed it was performing anything other than temporary military tasks in Asia. The United States has been preparing clients in Saigon to assume primary defense burdens since before Diem, with well-known consequences. Past experience with other Asian countries is hardly more encouraging. Recent congressional inquiries have revealed that it is impossible to determine exactly how much direct military aid the United States has provided its Asian allies since World War II, because of deliberate camouflaging of defense expenditures plus inept Pentagon accounting. Much military aid is also "indirect," in the form of equipment no longer used by American forces. And CIA budgets for military programs abroad are not revealed, even to Congress. A careful estimate advanced in 1971, however, concluded that in the past several decades the United States has spent in the neighborhood of $40–50 billion "to shore up East Asian client governments."[14]

A 1969 study of official aid calculated that between fiscal 1950 and fiscal 1968, over $9.7 billion in military equipment, training, and related support was

[13] Ibid., pp. 127–30.
[14] Ravenal, "The Political-Military Gap," p. 32.

made available to the countries of East and Southeast
Asia under the Military Assistance Program (MAP),
with South Korea ($2.5 billion) and Taiwan ($2.4
billion) the major recipients. Under MAP a total of
107,044 military personnel from Asia were trained in
the United States between 1950 and 1968. These included 28,525 from Korea, 15,280 from Japan, 23,113
from Taiwan, 12,217 from the Philippines, 10,136
from Thailand, and 13,998 from Vietnam. Between
1962 and 1968 a total of $1.4 billion worth of trans-
actions took place with the area under U.S. Foreign
Military Sales (FMS). The net total of economic and
military grants and loans between 1946 and 1968 for
the various countries (*after* repayments) runs along
these lines: Korea, $7.4 billion; Japan, $3.5 billion;
Taiwan, $4.9 billion; Philippines, $1.8 billion; Thailand, $1.1 billion. Breaking down the preceding fig-
ures for the military side only, one finds that between
1946 and 1968 the U.S. gave $12.7 billion in military
aid under SEATO (which would include Australia,
New Zealand, Thailand, and the Philippines) and
$2.8 billion to Taiwan, $1.1 billion to Japan, and
$2.8 billion to Korea.[15]

Such figures are conservative. The recent hearings
of the Joint Economic Committee under Senator
William Proxmire, for example, revealed that additional military aid has actually been effected under
guises as benign as the "Food for Peace" appropria-

[15] Congressional Quarterly Service, ed., *Global Defense:
U.S. Military Commitments Abroad* (Washington, D.C.: Government Printing Office, 1969).

tions; over $1.3 billion from this source alone has been used to provide military hardware for America's allies since the 1950s. Whatever the correct total figures, this aid has already spawned plump military establishments among America's major Asian allies. Japan's "self-defense" forces number around 275,000 men, an exceptionally high percentage of whom are officers and NCOs; Taiwan maintains the old retreating-trim of the Kuomintang at approximately 450,000; South Korea has roughly 620,000 men under arms; South Vietnam's military numbers 1.1 million (200,000 more than in 1968). The figures fall into a numbers game in which the President takes pride: "A decade ago our East Asian allies had about one million men under arms. Today that figure has more than doubled and the quality of equipment and training has significantly improved." But it is still not enough. On the contrary, the disengagement of American forces from Asia is being used by the President to justify much more of the same: "The Nixon Doctrine requires a strong program of security assistance. Today it is more important than ever, for without it our friends and allies cannot succeed."

Military aid has consistently cost more and accomplished less than anticipated. Similarly, Japan has always bulked largest in American projections for regional military and economic consolidation in Asia, and then failed to conform to expectations. Japan's potential as the pivot of power in Asia has been formally recognized by the U.S. at least since the National Security Council endorsed George

Kennan's report on Japan in 1948.[16] Beginning with Dulles, a familiar bogey of U.S. policy makers has been the allegation that Japan's industrial potential, if made available to the "communists," might decisively tip the "balance of world power." In January 1952, with the Japanese peace conference of the preceding September under his belt, Dulles struck the theme of military self-help among America's allies in Asia, led by Japan:

Our occupation policies, now crowned by a liberal peace, mean that Japan can soon emerge as an important factor in world defensive strategy against militant communism. That is the goal of our policy. There is dire need for more effective participation by the peoples of the East in the defense of freedom.[17]

Dulles' agitation for a rearmed Japan preceded the Korean War and postulated the creation of a Japanese military of between 300,000 and 350,000 men, capable of being dispatched beyond the home islands and assuming regional leadership in conventional defense against communism in Asia. American pressure upon Japan toward this goal has been fairly steady ever since, with Mr. Nixon himself playing an influential early role in popularizing the concept of a remilitarized Japan. As vice president in November 1953, he attracted front-page headlines by stating in

[16] See George F. Kennan, *Memoirs, 1925–1950*, chapter 16, for an interesting account of his role in bringing about the "reverse course" in American policy toward occupied Japan.

[17] *Department of State Bulletin*, April 9, 1951, p. 576; and January 21, 1951, p. 91.

Tokyo that the United States "made a mistake in 1946" when it disarmed Japan and sponsored the adoption of Article 9, the "no-war" clause of the new Japanese constitution. An excerpt from the *New York Times* coverage of this famous speech gives some idea of how dated Mr. Nixon's "new" Doctrine actually is:

"The United States cannot do the job alone. All the free nations of the world must stand together.

"It is essential for the United States to have friends. What happens in Asia is just as important as what happens in Europe."

Mr. Nixon described Japan as "a key bastion for the defense of Asia."

"If Japan falls, all of Asia falls," he continued. "Likewise, if Asia falls, Japan falls, too."

"Japan must work with the free nations, maintaining adequate strength."[18]

Secretary Laird's well-publicized visit to Tokyo in

[18] *New York Times,* November 19, 1953. American military policy toward Japan prior to the Korean War is discussed in John W. Dower, "The Eye of the Beholder: Background Notes on the U.S.-Japan Military Relationship," *Bulletin of Concerned Asian Scholars,* Vol. II, No. 1 (October 1969), and also in "Occupied Japan and the American Lake, 1945–1950" by the same author in Edward Friedman and Mark Selden, eds., *America's Asia: Dissenting Essays in Asian-American Relations* (New York: Pantheon, 1970). See also Burton Sapin, "The Role of the Military in Formulating the Japanese Peace Treaty," in Gordon B. Turner, ed., *A History of Military Affairs in Western Society since the Eighteenth Century* (New York: Harcourt Brace Jovanovich, Inc., 1952), and the initial sections of a complacent work by Martin Weinstein, *Japan's Postwar Defense Policy* (New York: Columbia University Press, 1970).

July 1971 belonged to this continuum of American pressure for a more militarily active Japan. So, too, do recent American suggestions that Japan join an international police force in Indochina or prepare its navy to police the Taiwan Straits or engage in more integrated security planning with South Korea and Taiwan.

In the same 1953 speech Nixon also touched upon an economic theme which has reemerged (as "multi-nationalism") in the Nixon Doctrine. "The United States," he stated, "is concerned with finding means of expanding trade between Japan and the other areas of the world, particularly Southeast Asia." A month later Nixon explained the subtle relationship between Japan, Southeast Asia, and America's Asia policy in greater detail:

Why is the United States spending hundreds of millions of dollars supporting the forces of the French Union in the fight against communism? If Indo-China falls, Thailand is put in an almost impossible position. The same is true of Indonesia. If this whole part of Southeast Asia goes under Communist domination or Communist influence, Japan, who trades and must trade with this area in order to exist, must inevitably be oriented towards the Communist regime.[19]

At a press conference on April 7, 1954, a month before the French defeat at Dienbienphu, President Eisenhower expressed a similar view. According to the stenographic record:

[19] *Department of State Bulletin,* January 4, 1954.

In its economic aspects, the President added, loss of Indochina would take away that region that Japan must have as a trading area, or it would force Japan to turn toward China and Manchuria, or toward the Communist areas in order to live. The possible consequences of the loss of Japan to the free world are just incalculable, Mr. Eisenhower said.[20]

Dulles made the same connection exactly a month later. Ho Chi Minh, he declared, was a "communist . . . trained in Moscow" who would "deprive Japan of important foreign markets and sources of food and raw materials."[21]

The United States has encouraged Japan's economic involvement in Southeast Asia since the Korean War. The reasons are complex, as the quotations above suggest—a mixture of economics, communism, and dominoes. Behind this encouragement was the "loss" of China coupled with a grudging postwar acknowledgment of Japan's extraordinary industrial potential. This "reverse course" in American policy toward occupied Japan, which began in 1947–1948, reflected the realization that Japan rather than China would become the key to American interests in Asia, and thereafter the task became one of fixing Japan firmly in the American camp. American bases in Japan and Japanese rearmament represent the military side of this policy. At the same time Japan was

[20] Cited in Carl Oglesby and Richard Shaull, *Containment and Change* (New York: Macmillan, 1967), p. 128.

[21] United Kingdom, Secretary of State for Foreign Affairs, *Documents Relating to British Involvement in the Indochina Conflict, 1945–1965*, pp. 66–67.

diverted from its intention of ultimately extending diplomatic recognition to the Chinese mainland government and restoring economic relations with the continent, a policy calculated to: (1) deprive China of the benefits of trade with an industrialized and technologically more advanced Japan; (2) prevent Japan from becoming close to or in any way dependent upon communist neighbors; (3) enhance America's commercial position vis-à-vis Japan; (4) make economic plasma available through Japan to the faltering anticommunist regimes in Southeast Asia; and thus (5) further integrate Southeast Asia into the capitalist system and effectively bar it from trading with China.[22] The economic dimension of the Nixon Doctrine—that is, the U.S.-Japan-Southeast Asia nexus—is thus interlocked with both past perceptions and present economic containment of China. As described below, this is also a dimension in which great tensions are now emerging.

The continuities between American policy formulations in the 1950s and 1960s and those of the present

[22] See for example Oglesby and Shaull, *Containment and Change*, pp. 121–130; also Gunnar Adler-Karlsson, *Western Economic Warfare 1947–1967: A Case Study in Foreign Economic Policy*, Acta Universitatis Stockholmienses, Stockholm Economic Studies, New Series IX (Stockholm, 1968), especially the introduction and chapter 16. Japan's intention to establish some sort of relations with the People's Republic of China, and American pressure forcing her away from this policy, are noted in several Japanese works relating to the postwar Japanese prime minister Shigeru Yoshida, including his *Nihon to sekai* (Japan and the World) and the comprehensive official publication covering his five terms up to 1954 *Yoshida naikaku* (The Yoshida Cabinets).

day thus run in deeper and potentially more destructive channels than defenders of the Nixon Doctrine acknowledge. Where present policy departs from the past most notably is in the more pessimistic view now held of American military and economic capabilities, as well as in the new surrogate approaches being advanced to compensate for this weakness. Mr. Nixon's right-wing credentials have also defused the situation of opposition accusations of "retreat" and being "soft on communism," which he himself fostered in the early cold-war period and in all likelihood would be voicing today were he out of power. Still, the fact remains that the key formulations of the Nixon Doctrine would have been widely endorsed by the gamut of policy makers who encouraged and planned American intervention in Indochina over the past decades. Following the first State of the World message of February 18, 1970, for example, Max Frankel noted that "Mr. Nixon's aides concede . . . that there is nothing in his new doctrine that excludes a Dominican-style intervention in defense of vital interests. They say that the document is a call to the nation and Government to define those interests more precisely and prudently than in the past, but they have only begun that job and it is never really finished until the moment of crisis."[23] That the misguided Dominican intervention should be cited as the example of defense of American "vital interests," however, offers little hope for a reasoned American response to those

[23] *New York Times,* February 19, 1970.

"moments of crisis" which will surely arise in the future.

II

The new China policy, dramatic and significant as it is, has been accompanied by reaffirmation of the containment policy and recommitment to the objectives of "anticommunism" and counterrevolution throughout Asia. Dictated to a considerable extent by extraordinary economic pressures upon the President, both domestic and international, it is being developed within the old "containment without isolation" formula. American forward bases in Asia are not being abandoned. Despite new public emphasis upon China's defensive orientation, Secretary Laird's view that China poses "a pervading psychological and actual threat to the peace and security of the Asian arena" remains a bedrock of U.S. policy, and the United States continues to define its objectives insofar as allied countries on China's periphery are concerned in terms of military containment. As noted in the 1971 Defense Report, the American objective in Asia is "for our Asian friends and allies to strengthen their conventional forces, both to defend themselves against non-Chinese attacks and, in regional conjunction, to build a defensive capability which would give Communist China increased pause before initiating hostilities." At the same time Laird also suggested that "an area ballistic missile defense effective against small attacks" be developed to supplement America's already immense nuclear superiority vis-à-vis the Chinese.[24]

Focus on the new China policy, moreover, has tended to obscure the fact that no new policies have been advanced which reflect a revised understanding and appreciation of the needs and internal dynamics of the countries of Asia. U.S. policy remains grounded in a negative and mechanistic response toward a stereotyped conception of insurgency and antiforeign movements. That stereotype, of course, is also intertwined with an image of China's role in "wars of liberation" in Asia. While the military effectiveness of the insurgency movements of Indochina can no longer be denied, the humanitarian goals, political and social competence, and popular support of the NLF and Pathet Lao (a sharp contrast to the narrowly based, corrupt, and inefficient regimes the U.S. supports against them) have not been acknowledged and used as the basis for a truly fundamental policy reappraisal. Opposition to popular revolutionary movements in Asia remains central to the Nixon Doctrine. Again in Laird's words:

The principal threat to the independent nations in Asia is internal insurgency supported by external assistance. This is an important aspect of the threat to which our General Purpose Force planning for Asia should be oriented.[25]

[24] *Hearings*, p. 2331.
[25] *Defense Industry Bulletin*, April 1970, p. 22. The statement appears in Laird's presentation of the Pentagon's budget request for fiscal 1971.

In fact, the principal threat to independence and social and economic progress in Asia is the existence of reactionary cliques propped up by American support. The assumption that internal insurrection is, by definition, negative in content and antithetical to American interests in Asia is the very seed of the tragedy of American policy in Asia. It gives the lie to professions of respect for national aspirations, for it denies a priori an entire spectrum of legitimate popular expression. In practice, the new "dialogue" means little more than continued consultation with American-created or American-financed elites. The U.S. continues to attempt to shape internal developments among its Asian allies in accordance with American desires. It is the buildup of huge client armies fashioned in the traditional "anticommunist" mold of the cold war, and not popular initiatives and aspirations, which Washington hopes will shape Asia's destiny.

Finally, it must be emphasized that the notion that American "interests" in Asia may in the future require U.S. intervention on the *local or subtheater* level has not been rejected. On the contrary, it has been explicitly reemphasized, and the possibility of committing American ground forces to such local Asian conflicts in the future has also been reaffirmed. In the President's curiously ambiguous words:

No President can guarantee that future conflicts will never involve American personnel—but in some theaters the threshold of involvement will be raised and in some in instances the threshold of involvement will be much more unlikely.

As Laird explained it:

In deterring subtheater or localized warfare, the country
or ally which is threatened bears the primary burden
particularly for providing manpower; but when U.S.
interests or obligations are at stake, we must be prepared
to provide help as appropriate through military and economic assistance to those nations willing to assume their
share of responsibility for their own defense. When required and appropriate, this help would consist essentially of backup logistical support and sea and air combat
support. In some special cases, it could include ground
combat support as well.[26]

If national interests are still considered to rise or
fall with local military situations in Asia, the United
States can hardly be regarded as having left the era
of Dienbienphu.

III

*American "military disengagement" from Asia is
being carried out only in a limited way; what is
actually taking place is a rationalization of troop
commitments and consolidation of the network of
forward American bases.* First it must be noted that
"disengagement" involves primarily ground combat
troops, while support forces, especially air power,
will remain. This is openly acknowledged. In his
budget report for fiscal 1972, Laird observed that
"with regard to U.S. force capabilities in Asia, we do
not plan for the long term to maintain separate large
U.S. ground combat forces specifically oriented just

[26] *Hearings*, p. 2333; see also pp. 2390, 2518, 2564, 2607–
2608.

to this theater, but we do intend to maintain strong air, naval and support capabilities."[27]

In Vietnam itself, despite official denials, there is little reason to believe that the United States seriously envisions anything other than, at a minimum, a variety of the "Korean solution" in which a residual American force is indefinitely maintained in key bases for the forseeable future. The Laos invasion dramatized what has long been obvious: the South Vietnamese military (ARVN) is being encouraged to prolong the anticommunist crusade in Indochina, and it is completely incapable of functioning effectively without massive American support. American helicopters and B-52s are playing an increasingly heavy role as bombing substitutes for the ineffective ARVN, and Air Force C-13s have recently resorted to seven and a half ton bombs (capable of causing internal hemorraging in anyone within one mile of the explosion). According to a November 1971 study prepared under Cornell University's Center for International Studies, more bomb tonnage has already been dropped on Indochina during the first three years of the Nixon administration (2.916 million tons) than during the previous five years of the Johnson administration (2.865 million tons). The new combination is ominous. Since half a million American troops plus the most intense bombing in history have already failed to achieve "victory," it is not likely that more bombing plus worse troops will do better. The likelihood of military embarrassment in-

[27] *Hearings,* p. 2368.

creases in direct proportion to the commitment to "Vietnamization," suggesting that unless America's overall goals are changed a point of instability will be reached in Indochina when the alternatives appear to be either defeat, indefinite and devastating military stalemate, or technological escalation.

There is every indication that the U.S. will also maintain the most critical of the nearly 200 *major* bases it maintains elsewhere in Asia. Some are being phased out as obsolete or uneconomical. Tachikawa in Japan is a recent example. Others are being turned over to local forces for maintenance, as has been noted recently in Japan, Okinawa, and Vietnam. But there is no intention of abandoning the strategy of forward American bases in Asia. Announcements of the elimination of U.S. military "installation" must be heard with the awareness that often these are golf courses, firing ranges, or the like, and also with a recognition of the immensity of the physical presence of the American military in Asia. At the time the President announced his doctrine on Guam, American bases in Asia officially classified as "major" totaled 54 in Korea, 40 in Japan, 16 in Okinawa, 3 in Taiwan, 6 in the Philippines, 7 in Thailand, and 9 in Micronesia (the Marianas, Marshall Island, and Midway). The accepted number of major bases in Vietnam is close to 60.[28] As of mid-1971, American troop deployment in Asia was approximately as follows: 43,000 in Korea; 50,000 in Okinawa; 35,000

[28] Statistics primarily from Congressional Quarterly, Inc., *Global Defense* (September 1969).

in Japan; 32,000 in Thailand; 18,000 in the Philippines; and 9,000 in Taiwan. Including all services, over 210,000 American military personnel were in Vietnam. Naval and Marine personnel with the Pacific Fleet totaled some 240,000; 65,000 Americans were with the Seventh Fleet.

Obviously it will be possible to trim an impressive amount of fat without touching the real bones of the American military posture toward Asia. Moreover even as certain facilities are being closed or cut back, other major Asian bases are being expanded and new sites and facilities acquired. In two perceptive articles, Michael Klare has suggested that among the key bases which will probably assume a pivotal role in post-Vietnam strategic planning are the huge logistical bases at Cam Ranh Bay (South Vietnam) and Sattahip (Thailand); the air force complexes at Tan Son Nhut (Saigon) and U-Taphao and Khorat (Thailand); and probably counterinsurgency or paramilitary centers such as those located at Nhatrang (South Vietnam), Kanchanaburi and Udorn (Thailand), and Vientiane (Laos).[29]

The Philippines, Japan, and Guam remain of central importance to Pacific planning; they house, in addition to major air fields and supply depots, the four major naval facilities used by the Seventh Fleet (Guam, Subic Bay in the Philippines, Sasebo and Yokosuka in Japan). The $2 billion American

[29] See footnote 6 above and also Klare's article "The Sun Never Sets on America's Empire: U.S. Bases in Asia," *Commonweal*, May 22, 1970.

complex on Okinawa, with 120 separate military installations on this island alone, poses particular problems because its use up to now as a site for nuclear MACE-B missiles (specially designed against China), as a berth for nuclear-armed Polaris submarines, and as a storage arsenal for nuclear bombs probably will be modified when sovereignty over the island reverts to Japan in 1972. Several fallback sites have been suggested as alternatives to handle Okinawa's present nuclear functions. Most frequently mentioned is the Mariana island chain, which includes Guam and Saipan. Other options which have been suggested are South Korea and Thailand; in the fall of 1970 it was revealed that the U.S. had already shifted virtually all of its B-52 operations from Okinawa to Thailand.

At the time of the initial announcement of the Nixon Doctrine in 1969, the four main islands of Japan housed over 125 U.S. military installations, of which 28 Army, 6 Navy, and 6 Air Force were classified as "major." Many of these will continue to be utilized by the U.S. Navy and Air Force, with the Japanese military gradually assuming a more direct role in their upkeep during the 1970s. In the summer of 1970, Yasuhiro Nakasone, Director General of the Japanese Self-Defense Agency, revealed that joint Japanese-American control of U.S. bases in Japan was already being implemented, and will involve major as well as minor installations. At about the same time, Colonel Thomas L. Murphy, commander of the huge Kadena Air Force Base on Okinawa, announced that the U.S. is planning a $60 million program on Okinawa to carry through fiscal 1976. This will include improved facilities for American servicemen and their dependents, in addition to new projects such as a sentry-dog training center and facilities for the new jumbo C-5A transport plane. In Colonel Murphy's words, the announcement was made to "give some encouragement" to Okinawan businessmen whose livelihood is entirely dependent on the continued U.S. military presence. According to the *New York Times*, the projects "are said to be directed at turning Okinawa into a more important strategic bastion after the Vietnam war is over."[30] The U.S.-Japan agreement on Okinawan reversion, ratified in November 1971, assures American retention of the vast network of military bases.

In the Indian Ocean the thrust of American concerns seems to imply not continued disengagement, but rather the assumption of new missions. In January 1969 Britain announced that it would withdraw its troops east of Suez by the end of 1971, thus threatening to leave what Western geopoliticians refer to as a "power vacuum" in the Indian Ocean—a term commonly used here to mean an absence of Anglo-Saxons. The most dramatic recent example of U.S. military activity in this area was the controversial entry of the world's largest nuclear-powered aircraft carrier, the USS *Enterprise*, with a nine-ship escort into the Indian Ocean during the India-Pakistan War. Long before this, however, the "vacuum,"

[30] *New York Times*, August 5 and July 5, 1970.

coupled with recent expansion of Soviet naval strength, had been cited by administration advisers who seek the creation of a permanent U.S. task force in the Indian Ocean. Steps have already been taken to increase U.S. naval capabilities in the area. Probably of greatest significance are the sophisticated communications facilities being established at Northwest Cape (Australia), Canterbury (New Zealand), and Asmara (Ethiopia), which together will provide the electronic network necessary for operations in the entire Indian Ocean area. As Klare has pointed out, the Australian facility, one of the largest in the world, will house the most powerful VLF (very low frequency) transmitter in existence, which will function as part of the "Omega" system for radio transmission with submerged nuclear submarines.[31]

On the eastern rim of the South Asian theater interest is also focused on the future disposition of the great naval facilities in Singapore, which Britain has already turned over to the Singapore government. In keeping with the new soft-shoe approach to military choreography in Asia, a 1969 issue of the *Naval War College Review* offered this suggestion concerning Singapore:

U.S. interest in that excellent facility, if deemed feasible, should be approached in low-profile, and negotiations for U.S. interests could be pursued through its allies such as Japan or Australia, both of whom have principal interests there. Arrangements could provide for joint utilization

[31] Klare discusses this in both of the articles mentioned above. Cf. *New York Times*, May 1, 1969.

on a cost- and maintenance-sharing basis. The availability of this facility would provide a superior logistical capability for the U.S. Navy than it has at present.[32]

Whatever form the future American military presence may take in Asia, the essentials of the containment policy remain. The Seventh Fleet will continue to prowl Asia's shores. Polaris submarines will continue to glide beneath the Pacific, systematically undergoing a sea-change to the "Poseidon configuration."[33] SAC will continue to be guaranteed runways

[32] Murray Marks, "Southeast Asia: Strategic Alternatives after Vietnam," *Naval War College Review* (May 1969), p. 97; Marks is a colonel at the U.S. Air Force School of Naval Warfare. In his January 1970 tour of Asia, Vice President Spiro Agnew indicated that a "definite relationship" on the part of the U.S. was also in the offing. The U.S. Navy is known to be interested in access to both the dockyard and aircraft maintenance shops in Singapore, as well as to the morale-boosting recreational facilities of this famous port of call. At the present time there appear to be no plans for establishing formal American air or naval bases in the area, but a number of "private" American defense contractors, particularly Lockheed, have shown considerable interest in collaborating with the Singapore government in developing an aerospace industry utilizing the excellent existing facilities at Singapore's three air bases (Tengah, Seletar, and Changi). The Singapore government itself engaged the Washington consulting firm Murphy Mundy Associates—which is closely associated with the aerospace and defense industries—to investigate the prospects of such development (*New York Times*, July 6, 1969).

[33] The Poseidon configuration consists of MIRVing the missiles on the Polaris submarines. There are forty-one Polaris nuclear submarines, each carrying sixteen missiles. Thirty-one submarines in the fleet are being refitted to the Poseidon missile, which will provide ten warheads per missile. As stated in testimony before the House Armed Services Committee, "The number of independently targetable warheads on this force is thus rising from 656 to over 5,000 as the force is retro-fitted" (*Hearings*, pp. 2780–2781).

which will permit it to rain destruction from the skies. Asian real estate will continue to be made available for American storage and positioning of conventional weapons, missiles, nuclear devices, gases, poisons, vehicles, computers, provisions, and other items required to eradicate Asians should the occasion arise. Meanwhile, elsewhere, one thousand ICBMs will continue to nestle in their silos, gradually being "MIRV'd" and awaiting the turn of the key.

IV

"Asianization" means continued and even intensified involvement in the creation of client armies which are to fight in defense of America's interests in Asia. "Vietnamization," under which the South Vietnamese Army is now being financed and trained to continue the war, is the primary model of the Nixon Doctrine in action. Similarly, the unleashing of South Vietnamese troops in Cambodia "to assure the survival of the Government of Lon Nol in Phnomphenh and prevent the return to power of Prince Sihanouk" was justified by Secretary of State Rogers on the grounds that "the whole Nixon Doctrine as pronounced at Guam is that Asians should work with each other to take care of their common problems."[34] In this case, the most obvious common problem shared by Lon Nol and the South Vietnamese government was that neither had much popular support. The subsequent invasion of Laos followed a similar pattern,

[34] *New York Times,* May 15, 1970.

making amply clear that American "disengagement" from Southeast Asia does not imply American restraint from the encouragement of military adventures in this area.

Despite the fact that the 1.1 million-man ARVN has been wet-nursed by the United States for over a decade and still cannot hold its own without American air and combat support against numerically and technologically inferior NLF and North Vietnamese forces, this appears to be the path of the future for America's allies: more U.S. military aid (note the accelerating commitment to the Lon Nol regime in Cambodia); more U.S. military advisers (witness the new John F. Kennedy Center for Military Assistance at Fort Bragg);[35] more military training for Asian nationals (Thai soldiers, for example, receive CBW training in the U.S. in preparation for the day when they too can participate in the defoliation of their land);[36] a larger policy-making role for the Pentagon and CIA (this seems to be the implication of the recent proposal to turn AID functions over to the Pentagon);[37] emphasis upon police functions and control mechanisms within the client society (close to 50 percent of the "civilian" aid budget to Thailand, for example, is now being spent on police

[35] *New York Times*, June 10 and 11, 1970.

[36] *Congressional Record*, November 29, 1970. The "small arms training" of Indonesian soldiers at the Institute for Technical Interchange of Hawaii's East-West Center is reported in John Witeck "The East-West Center: An Intercult of Colonialism," *Hawaii Pono Journal*, Special Issue (1971), pp. 39–40.

[37] *New York Times*, June 10, 1970.

stations and specially trained Special Police);[38] and so on. In effect, the U.S. seeks to defend its ambitions in Asia through proxy armies and client regimes.

There is little new in this approach. In various forms military aid has comprised the preponderant part of U.S. aid to Asia throughout the postwar era, despite the often humanistic rhetoric of "nation building." South Korea, heralded as "the first application of the so-called Nixon Doctrine aside from Indochina," can be taken as a case in point. In June, 1970, the Defense Department announced that over the course of the next few years, the U.S. intended to withdraw all but a token contingent of its 63,000 troops (53,000 Army and 10,000 Air Force) then stationed in South Korea. This was subsequently reduced following expressions of concern on the part of the South Korean government, but the U.S. has already withdrawn roughly one-third of its forces. They leave behind over 40,000 American troops, a 620,000-man South Korean military establishment, a projected paramilitary "home guard" of two million men, and a U.S.-funded squadron (around 54 planes) of Phantom F-40 fighter-bombers. In addition, Washington has promised the South Korean government more than one and a half billion dollars in military aid and equipment over the next five years to be used in further modernizing the Korean military. While South Korea will not be provided with its own air sufficiency (partly because it is feared that the Seoul government will then attack the North), bids have

[38] Cf. Klare, "The Great South Asian War," p. 4.

been opened to American defense contractors for a proposed short-range jet fighter appropriate for use by Korea and other allies such as Taiwan and Thailand; some $28 million for such a study was made available by the U.S. government in fiscal 1970, and another $30 million was requested for fiscal 1971. In addition, the United States has privately agreed to advance credits for the construction of a factory to manufacture M-16 rifles.[39]

As an example of regional military cooperation, South Korea has sent 50,000 troops to Vietnam at an estimated cost to American taxpayers of $1 billion since 1965. The South Koreans in Vietnam (like the South Vietnamese in Cambodia) have distinguished themselves by their brutality; they have been charged with carrying out systematic atrocities by a number of journalists, as well as by researchers under contract to RAND Corporation and the Defense Department.[40]

In his 1970 State of the World address, the President cited South Korea as an example of regional development and Asian capitalist prosperity. In his words, "Korea's annual growth rate of 15 per cent may be the highest in the world." He neglected to note that, in the first place, Korea's boom since 1965 has been intimately tied in to war profits derived from Korean exports to Vietnam, fees to Korean

[39] Laird uses the Korean situation to illustrate the Asian-soldier-is-cheaper-than-an-American-soldier argument, and argues that the one and a half billion appropriation for Korea will save American taxpayers close to a half billion dollars over the course of the five years. Cf. *Hearings*, p. 2392.

[40] *New York Times*, January 10, 11, 12, and 16, 1970.

civilian contractors there, dollar remittances from the earnings of the 50,000 American-paid Korean soldiers and 16,000 Korean civilians employed by the U.S. in Vietnam, and direct and indirect earnings from the American military presence in South Korea itself. In 1969, an estimated twenty percent of South Korea's foreign currency revenue came from Vietnam.[41]

The second great stimulus to Korea's economic growth has been the influx of Japanese capital since the conclusion of the Korea-Japan normalization pact of 1965. Ostensibly another positive illustration of regional self-help, in fact the Japanese thrust has already severely compromised South Korea's economic independence and represents a significant step backward in the direction of the colonial relationship which existed between the two countries from 1910–1945.

"Koreanization," like "Vietnamization," is a cover phrase for militarization and neocolonial relationships. And it is a striking commentary upon both the Nixon Doctrine and its apologists that the two Asian client states which have been most distorted by American policy in the past are now blandly offered as models for the future.

V

American planners also believe that the reduction of American forces in Asia can be compensated for by new military technology. While Asian land forces

[41] *New York Times,* January 26, 1970.

will assume some of the burden left by the withdrawal of American manpower, a less propagandized but potentially more significant surrogate development lies in the new technology of death now under development. Several years ago it was calculated that thirteen new weapons systems were already "waiting in the Pentagon wings" and scheduled for production following the termination of hostilities in Indochina.[42] Of particular interest insofar as the Nixon Doctrine is concerned are two rather dramatized projects: (1) the concept of rapid transport and the fire brigade, first popularized by Secretary of Defense Robert McNamara; and (2) the electronic battlefield recently rhapsodized by General Westmoreland.

McNamara explained his concept of rapid transport and brushfire wars as follows in 1965:

Either we can station large numbers of men and quantities of equipment and supplies overseas near all potential trouble spots, or we can maintain a much smaller force in a central reserve in the United States and deploy it rapidly where needed. . . . A mobile "fire brigade" reserve, centrally located . . . and ready for quick deployment to any threatened area in the world, is, basically, a more economical and flexible use of our military forces.[43]

One key to the brushfire concept lies in the new capabilities of air transport, primarily as exemplified in the now notorious C-5A. Six stories tall and nearly as long as a football field (dubbed "Moby Jet" by a

[42] Richard Barnet, *The Economy of Death* (New York: Atheneum, 1968).

[43] Quoted in Klare, "The Great South Asian War," p. 7.

metaphysical PR man), each of these superjets can
carry 600 men and their equipment, or the equivalent
of this. The plane is also capable of taking off and
landing on short runways, thus enabling it to set
down almost anywhere. In addition, it is equipped
with lifts, ramps, and the like which make it "self-un
loading," thus permitting use of poorly equipped
airfields. The supertransport is a key component of
what is known to military planners as "rapid deployment strategy" or "rapid response capability." It
has been described by high officials as the pivot of
logistics planning for the decade of the 1970s. One
Air Force officer, speaking informally, has likened
the C-5A to an advanced form of gunboat diplomacy.
Lockheed, the manufacturer, advertises its product in
these terms:

The C-5A Galaxy is more than the world's largest airplane.
It's a new kind of defense system. It's like having a military base in nearly every strategic spot on the globe.

Senator Stuart Symington, whose concern about
threats to the supremacy of the dollar and opposition
to reliance on U.S. ground forces in Asia has gained
him something of a reputation as a "dove," defended
funding of the C-5A on grounds which neatly sum
up the crucial relationship between the transport
revolution and the Nixon policy of "disengagement":

I want to say here and now, that people who really mean
it when they say we should bring these troops home, had
better provide for the airlift because you are not going to

be able to bring them home until you have some means to send them back.[44]

Sixty-five C-5As will be active within a year, with a total of eighty-one planned before the end of fiscal 1973.[45] In the meantime, the Navy is engaged in prototype developments which it hopes will result eventually in comparable rapid sealift capabilities. The projected "100-knot Navy" of the future was discussed in the 1972 House hearings on military posture:

Chairman This ship of the future, this 100-knot ship is, of course, a fantastic thing. It is almost like going into a dream at this time. That is the reason I wanted you to explain it to the committee. The first test will be on the 100-ton. I think that is projected to [deleted] knots, isn't it?

Admiral Zumwalt Yes, sir.

Chairman Then you visualize the potential of the future that you would go to finally a 90- and a 100-knot ship, and that would be represented by [deleted].

Admiral Zumwalt This is correct, sir.

Chairman Which, of course, is a fantastic thing, and you visualize, too, in this future Navy, the delivery of personnel and armament, in probably one-tenth of the time it would take today?

Admiral Zumwalt Yes, sir.[46]

Just as new potentialities of transportation make it possible to reevaluate the entire concept of per-

[44] Quoted in *I. F. Stone's Weekly*, September 22, 1969. For an overall treatment of the C-5A see Berkeley Rice, *The C-5A Scandal: An Inside Story of the Military-Industrial Complex* (Boston: Houghton-Mifflin, 1971).

[45] *Hearings*, p. 2383. See also pp. 2604–2606 on the C-5A.

[46] *Hearings*, pp. 2697–2698.

manent garrisons abroad without necessarily reevaluating commitments or definitions of "national security" or "interest," so in a similar manner new developments in tactical warfare may make it possible to kill on the old scale and for the old goals but with new and impersonal dispatch. As American troops are withdrawn from Asia their place will be taken by America's client armies, with the menacing presence of Moby Jet ever in the background. But that is only half of it. General Westmoreland evokes a vision of a time when it may be possible to respond militarily to Asia's protesting peasants largely by computer and the touch of a few select buttons.

Like the concept of the fire brigade, the "electronic battlefield" also had its inspiration during the McNamara tenure. It derives from studies undertaken in 1966 by the Institute for Defense Analyses for creation of an "electronic fence" for Vietnam—the so-called McNamara Wall—and some of its components have been tested and used in Vietnam, Laos, and Cambodia since 1968. Its potential is sufficient to quicken the prose of even as stiff and prosaic a warrior as Westmoreland, as witness the General's classic address of October 14, 1969, on "The Army of the Future":

In mid 1968, our field experiments began . . . we are on the threshold of an entirely new battlefield concept. . . . On the battlefield of the future, enemy forces will be located, tracked, and targeted almost instantaneously through the use of data links, computer assisted intelligence evaluation, and automated fire control. With first round kill probabilities approaching certainty, and with surveillance devices that can continually track the enemy, the need for large forces to fix the opposition physically will be less important.

. . . Based on our total battlefield experience and our proven technological capability, I foresee a new battlefield array.

I see new battlefields on which we can destroy anything we locate through instant communications and the almost instantaneous application of highly lethal firepower.

I see a continuing need for highly mobile combat forces to assist in fixing and destroying the enemy.

The changed battlefield will dictate that the supporting logistics system also undergo change. . . .

I see the forward end of the logistics system with mobility equal to the supported force.

I see the elimination of many intermediate support echelons and the use of inventory-in-motion techniques.

I see some Army forces supported by air—in some instances directly from bases here in the continental United States.

. . . With cooperative effort, no more than 10 years should separate us from the automated battlefield.[47]

A similar breathless description of the battlefield of the future was offered around the same time

[47] *Congressional Record*, October 16, 1969. The speech was delivered to the Association of the United States Army and entered into the *CR* by Senator Barry Goldwater. See also chapter 7 of Committee of Concerned Asian Scholars, ed., *The Indochina Story*. A more technical description appears in DMS (Defense Market Service), *Market Intelligence Reports*, "Electronic Battlefield" (New York: McGraw-Hill, November 1969).

(August 1969) by the Deputy Director of Research and Development for South East Asian Matters, Leonard Sullivan:

These developments open up some very exciting horizons as to what we can do five or ten years from now: When one realizes that we can detect anything that perspires, moves, carries metal, makes a noise, or is hotter or colder than its surroundings, one begins to see the potential. This is the beginning of instrumentation of the entire battlefield. Eventually, we will be able to tell when anybody shoots, what he is shooting at, and where he was shooting from. You begin to get a "Year 2000" vision of an electronic map with little lights that flash for different kinds of activity. This is what we require for this "porous" war, where the friendly and the enemy are all mixed up together.

At the same time, in a comparably mechanistic view of the problems and aspirations of the peoples of Southeast Asia, Mr. Sullivan related the new technology to the issue of future insurgency in Indochina:

If all the smoke were cleared away, if we stopped the bombing of the North, if the North Vietnamese stopped infiltrating into the South, if we stopped fighting main unit actions in the jungles, we would still have the problem of controlling the guerrilla. Who is the guerrilla? He is simply the local dissident or the local zealot. He is willing to commit acts of violence in order to make himself heard and in order to change his lot and that of future generations. The threshold of his violence is a fine balance between the strength of his discontent and his view of the consequences of his violence. We should be able to change an insurgent's threshold of violence by adjusting both sides of the balance. We can lower his level of discontent by peaceful action, and we can raise the apparent deterrent by suitable military or police presence —and technology can probably help on both sides.[48]

A year later, Senator Proxmire pointed out that $2 billion worth of research had still not made the electronic detection system capable of sorting out the friendly and the enemy on the battlefield of the future:

. . . the sensors could not differentiate between friend and foe, women and children.

All we know is that something is moving out there. It could be the wind, an elephant or an enemy soldier. We really have almost no idea what we are shooting at.[49]

For American military planners, however, that is probably not an entirely relevant concern. The fundamental principle of counterinsurgency which has emerged in the course of the war in Indochina is that of "emptying the countryside"—in military jargon, turning about the Chinese phrase: drying up the ocean of people in which the guerrillas move as fish. Drawing fine distinctions among "Oriental human beings" in the countryside has not been of particular importance previously, and there is no reason to expect it to become important in the future.

48 *Congressional Record,* August 11, 1969.
49 *Congressional Record,* August 17, 1970. See also *New York Times,* July 6 and 14, 1970.

What *is* important to the administration and military is the capability of killing more at less cost and less loss of American lives. A prototype system (SEEK DATA II) is already being installed in Vietnam, and Westmoreland suggests that instrumentation is indeed already taking over roles formerly requiring manpower:

Firepower can be concentrated without massing large numbers of troops. In Vietnam where artillery and tactical air forces inflict over two-thirds of the enemy casualties, firepower is responsive as never before. It can rain destruction anywhere on the battlefield within minutes . . . whether friendly troops are present or not.[50]

Dr. John S. Foster, Jr., Director of Defense Research and Engineering, notes that "each few years often sees a tenfold improvement" in military electronics technology, with these advances:

Flexibility of installation and operation and increased survivability will also be realized. New equipment will be considerably smaller in size, lighter in weight, more reliable, more easily maintained and, in some cases, less expensive. Greater power output will be possible with reduced power consumption.

Among the capabilities which it is hoped these developments will bring, Foster goes on to note that they may

Permit the development of ultrareliable equipment and systems (thousands vs. hundreds of hours between

[50] *Congressional Record,* October 16, 1969.

failures) that will drastically reduce supporting logistics costs (maintenance personnel, spare parts inventory, training) and increase operational availability.

Reduce the number of people overseas operating intelligence collection systems, thus reducing gold flow as well as certain risks in intelligence collection.[51]

The long-range economic benefits which proponents of the new technology commonly cite in defending their projects have not gone unchallenged. Senator Proxmire speculates that the automated battlefield alone may eventually carry a price tag in the neighborhood of $20 billion—in his words, "almost twice as much as we are spending on the ABM and four times as much as we have spent on the C-5A"[52] This is, of course, in addition to the development of more conventional new weapons systems for use in local or insurgency situations—new helicopters, fighter aircraft, tanks, missiles, etc. While both the C-5A and the electronic battlefield still pose technical problems, they nonetheless reveal that even without a "Nixon Doctrine," the logic of increasingly sophisticated military technology would have led toward a gradual "disengagement" of American manpower from Asia.

Where it will all end is anyone's guess, although those with a more macabre sense of destiny would

[51] *Defense Industry Bulletin,* May 1970. The statement comes from Dr. Foster's testimony before the Senate Joint Committee on Armed Services and Defense Subcommittee of the Appropriations Committee on February 26, 1970.

[52] *New York Times,* July 6, 1970.

seem to be on the right track. For example, Gordon J. F. MacDonald, a geophysicist and former vice president of the Institute for Defense Analyses, observed several years ago that man is already on the verge of being able to mass-produce drought, hurricanes, frost, and tidal waves, and may soon be able to create oscillating power fields "that would seriously impair brain performance in very large populations in selected regions over an extended period."[53] On a somewhat more familiar front, research applicable to chemical and biological warfare (CBW) continues in spite of widely publicized official statements to the contrary, beginning with President Nixon's announcement of November 25, 1969, that "The U.S. shall renounce the use of . . . all methods of biological warfare and will confine its biological research to defensive measures." Theatrical disposals of poisonous gases and dismissals of workers from key CBW installations such as Fort Dietrich, Maryland, and the Pine Bluff Arsenal in Arkansas have thrown a smokescreen over the continuation of CBW development. In April 1971, the Defense Marketing Survey (DMS), a private research service subscribed to primarily by defense contractors, informed its readers that "Despite public announcements to the contrary, the military agencies are not discontinuing chemical

[53] Cited in *New York Times Book Review*, July 28, 1968, in a review of Nigel Calder, ed., *Unless Peace Comes: A Scientific Forecast of New Weapons* (New York: Viking, 1968).

and biological warfare research. Work in these areas is continuing at funding levels equal to or exceeding those prior to the 'public relations' announcements of cessation of these efforts. CBW research is merely being conducted in a different environment, and wherever possible with less public attention." Contracts in the offing, according to DMS, include manufacture of nerve gases, incapacitating agents, riot control gases, harassing agents, defoliants, and herbicides, in addition to such biological agents as anthrax, plague, Rocky Mountain spotted fever, and tularemia.

CBW research is not merely continuing. In a recent U.S. military journal, a scientific article entitled "Ethnic Weapons" suggested that scientists may be able to circumvent one of the characteristics of biological warfare that has been a barrier to its use— the danger that a disease carrier released into the environment would be uncontrollable and could backfire on its user. According to Dr. Carl A. Larson, a Swedish geneticist, scientists are now beginning to sort out distinctive genetic patterns in different populations which make them particularly susceptible to certain diseases. In his words, "Although the study of drug metabolizing enzymes is only beginning, observed variations in drug response have pointed to the possibility of great innate differences in vulnerability to chemical agents between different populations." Major scientific discoveries in 1969, according to Dr. Larson, place the development of such agents within reach, thus raising the prospect that "forthcoming chemical agents with selective manstopping power will put into the hands of an assailant a weapon with which he cannot be attacked."[54]

In the summer of 1971, a group of scientists in the San Francisco area noted that floor plans for the new Western Institute of Medical Research, a $27 million military research facility now under construction at the Presidio army base, bear a close resemblance to the set-up at Fort Dietrich, and also that the new center will specialize in the study of "race-specific fungal diseases . . . endemic to Third World countries." Army spokesmen, on the other hand, deny the

[54] Dr. Larson is head of the Department of Human Genetics at the Institute of Genetics, University of Lund, Sweden; "Ethnic Weapons" appeared in the November 1970 issue of *Military Review*. Although the bulk of his article is comprised of a technical and sound survey of recent scientific advances, Dr. Larson occasionally veers off into a more murky realm of speculation. He concludes, for example, with this vision of potential battles of the future:

Another prospect may tempt an aggressor who knows he can recruit from a population largely tolerant against an incapacitating agent to which the target population is susceptible. An innate immunity would offer concealment of preparations and obvious advantages in many tactical situations. When the proper chemical agent is used against intermingled friendly and enemy units, casualties may occur in proportions one to ten.

Such inferences are barely extrapolations of observed genetic differences between major human populations and of research programs known to be in progress. Widely different opinions have been ventured as to the type of chemical operations likely to be directed against military personnel and the civilian population in a future war. There have been some recent tendencies to stress the wide latitude between incapacitating and the lethal action of BZ-type agents. Friendly troops could use them to dampen belligerence. They effectively slow down physical and mental activity, make the poisoned personnel giddy, disoriented, and more or less unable or unwilling to carry out commands.

CBW charges leveled at the new center and assert their concern is only with preventive medicine: "scientists will be investigating exotic diseases from out-of-the-way places all over the world, wherever American troops might be stationed."[55]

VI

The combination of old objectives, cost-consciousness, and reluctance to become mired in another counterinsurgency war in Asia increases the possibility of resort to nuclear weapons in the future. The nature of popular resistance to the military machines of the French and Americans over the past decades

---

Friendly forces would discriminatingly use incapacitants in entangled situations to give friend and foe a short period of enforced rest to sort them out. By gentle persuasion, aided by psychochemicals, civilians in enemy cities could be reeducated. The adversary would use incapacitants to spare those whom he could use for slaves. There is little that human biology can contribute to prognoses of that type.

The factual basis of absolute enzyme inhibitors of widely different types can be neglected as little as modern methods for their distribution. They need not be bases in a true sense. Well-studied enzymes represent a small proportion of the total number of catalysts necessary for our vital processes. When new enzyme varieties are discovered, some of them are likely to overstep the prevalence limits so far observed, both high and low, in different populations.

[55] On the present state of CBW research, particularly the issue of ethnic weapons and the controversy over the new Presidio research center, see the article by Martin Gallen and Elaine Elinson distributed in the summer of 1971 by Pacific News Service, 19 Sutter Street, San Francisco, California 94104); also the studies prepared by COMBAT (Coalition Opposed to Medical and Biological Attack, Suite 101, 1232 Market St., San Francisco, California 94102). The DMS and Larson Reports are cited in these sources.

in Indochina indicates that neither client armies nor American air and sea support nor supertransports nor still unperfected computerized battlefields will turn the tide decisively against future "insurgencies." At this point it becomes necessary to consider the role of the nuclear alternative in the Nixon Doctrine for Asia—keeping in mind the fact that, unlike many of the developments described in the previous sections, nuclear technology awaits no scientific breakthrough or additional billions for development. Nuclear weapons are highly perfected; they are deployed and battle-ready. Here it is instructive to recall Vice President Nixon's public position on the issue of nuclear weapons in 1955:

It is foolish to talk about the possibility that the weapons which might be used in the event war breaks out in the Pacific would be limited to the conventional Korean and World War II types of explosives. Our forces could not fight an effective war in the Pacific with those types of explosives if they wanted to. Tactical atomic explosives are now conventional and will be used against the military targets of any aggressive force.[56]

Among those who debate the issue, there is at the present time considerable disagreement as to whether or not the present leadership is more willing to consider the use of nuclear weapons in certain situations than has been the case in the past. Those who regard the possibility of the U.S. resorting to tactical nuclear

[56] March 17, 1955, in a speech to the Executive Club of Chicago. Quoted by Richard Barnet in *Hard Times,* May 25–June 1, 1970.

weapons as remote argue that world opinion would not tolerate it; that during the 1960s American military planners showed less interest in tactical nuclear weapons than in other weapons systems; that intolerable radiation levels plus undesirable wind patterns mitigate against the resort to nuclear weapons in Asia—particularly since prevailing winds might expose Japan to fallout; that once the barrier to use of nuclear weapons is violated, it is recognized that the potential for use elsewhere (for example the Middle East or Europe) is increased; and so on.

Such arguments are fairly persuasive if one assumes that pivotal military decisions are taken after careful deliberation—an assumption which hardly seems tenable any longer. Neither the President's past attitude toward nuclear weapons, his well-known pledge to "move decisively and not step by step" if challenged in Indochina,[57] his reliance upon advisers known to be especially tolerant of the "rational" use of tactical nuclear weapons in certain situations (Mr. Kissinger being the best known of these), nor his personal propensity for equating virility with force dispel this concern. In his second State of the World address on February 25, 1971, Mr. Nixon seemed to imply willingness to consider open-ended escalation with his observation that ". . . having a full range of options does not mean that we will necessarily limit our response to the level or intensity chosen by an enemy. Potential enemies must know that we will respond to whatever degree is required to protect our

[57] May 8, 1970.

interests." This same speech has been interpreted by one qualified observer as suggesting "the selective use of strategic nuclear weapons to achieve limited coercive or destructive purposes."[58] Secretary Laird, in his complementary Defense Report to the House Committee on Armed Services on March 9, 1971, noted that U.S. deterrence theory insofar as conventional theater war in Europe or Asia is concerned is predicated on the fact that "the Soviets and Chinese Communists cannot be sure that major conventional aggression would not be met with the tactical use of nuclear weapons." In phrases similar to the President's, he went on to reinforce the impression of U.S. willingness to escalate to the point of first use of tactical nuclear weapons:

. . . we must plan our theater nuclear weapon posture and relate it to our conventional posture in such a way that we have a realistic option in the theater without having to rely solely on strategic nuclear weapons. In other words, we plan to maintain tactical nuclear capabilities that contribute to realistic deterrence while allowing for maximum flexibility of response in every major contingency we plan for should deterrence fail.[59]

Precise information on present American nuclear deployment in Asia is difficult to come by. American use of Okinawa as a nuclear arsenal and site of nuclear missiles is widely known if not officialy acknowledge. Nuclear weapons are also maintained in

[58] The interpretation is Earl Ravenal's in "The Political-Military Gap," p. 36.
[59] *Hearings*, p. 2367.

Korea, Thailand, the Philippines, and within the Seventh Fleet. American tactical nuclear weapons teams in South Korea, for example, run regular monthly or bi-monthly "dry runs" of their missions, which include targets in *Seoul*. At the time of the Pueblo incident American fighter bombers stationed in South Korea were unable to respond immediately because they were equipped only with nuclear weapons. The most suggestive studies on these matters have emanated from the independent Institute for Policy Studies in Washington. Richard Barnet reports that as of 1968 the United States maintained more than 5,500 nuclear weapons in Southeast Asia, mostly on aircraft carriers, and that "Until 1965 the Commander in Chief of the Pacific (CINCPAC) had no plans or weapons capabilities to fight other than a nuclear war in Southeast Asia."[60]

The United States has publicly threatened and privately considered the use of nuclear weapons in Asia on a number of occasions since Hiroshima and Nagasaki. In December 1950 the staffs of both the Eighth Army and the Fifth Air Force debated using them in Korea.[61] Eisenhower threatened North Korea and China with atomic weapons in 1953 at the time of the Panmunjom negotiations. As he later informed Sherman Adams, "We told them we could not hold it to a limited war any longer if the Communists welched on a treaty of truce. They didn't want a full-

[60] *Hard Times*, May 25–June 1, 1970.

[61] *Air University Quarterly Review*, Vol. XII, No 1 (Spring 1960), p. 11.

scale war or an atomic attack. That kept them under some control. Adams also reported that the United States first moved atomic missiles to Okinawa in the spring of 1953, and that in May of the same year Dulles informed Nehru that if a truce could not be arranged in Korea, the U.S. could not be held responsible if it resorted to nuclear weapons.[62] In 1954, as the French faced defeat at Dienbienphu, the Joint Chiefs of Staff under Admiral Radford proposed an American atomic offensive if China intervened in Indochina, and then went on to state that even if China did not intervene, "The employment of atomic weapons is contemplated in the event that such a course appears militarily advantageous."[63] On March 15 and 16, 1955, Dulles and Eisenhower threatened China with retaliation by tactical nuclear weapons "in the event of a Communist Chinese attack on Quemoy and Matsu Islands in the Pacific."[64] During the even more intense Quemoy-Matsu crisis of 1958, a similar

[62] Adam's allegations appear in his book *First Hand Report: The Eisenhower Years* (New York: Harper & Row, 1961), pp. 48–49. Robert J. Donovan also reports the move of atomic missiles to Okinawa in 1953 in *Eisenhower—the Inside Story* (New York Harper & Row, 1956), p. 116. For these and several of the references which follow, I am indebted to a private communication from Professor Donald A. Geffen of the University of Minnesota. It should be noted that the interpretation that China backed down before America's nuclear blackmail —an interpretation very popular among deterrent theorists— is extremely dubious; see, for example, Edward Friedman, "The United States and China," in Steven L. Spiegel and Kenneth N. Waltz, eds., *Conflict in World Politics* (Cambridge, Mass.: Winthrop, 1971) pp. 55–77.

[63] *Pentagon Papers*, p. 46.

[64] *New York Times*, March 17, 1955. On March 16, Eisenhower was quoted as saying, "Now, in any combat where these things [tactical nuclear weapons] can be used on strictly

signal was again conveyed to China. At an Air Force Association banquet in Dallas on September 27, 1958, Secretary of the Air Force James H. Douglas noted the move of U.S. fighter-bombers to Taiwan, Okinawa, and the Philippines and stated: "So our most modern fighters are on the spot, ready to meet the threat of the Chinese Communists. And make no mistake, our fighter-bombers and light bombers are capable of using high-explosive bombs or more powerful weapons if necessary." This particular portion of Douglas's speech had originally been deleted by the State Department and then reinstated after a policy review.[65] That this was no idle threat is indicated by the fact that at the same time the U.S. provided the Chinese Nationalists on Quemoy with eight-inch howitzers and "indicated that they could event of a Communist Chinese attack on Quemoy have nuclear heads in them to wipe out the Chinese batteries on the mainland."[66] It has been widely

---

military targets and for strictly military purposes, I see no reason why they shouldn't be used just exactly as you would use a bullet or anything else." In the words of the *Times,* Eisenhower's statement "backed up the Secretary of State, John Foster Dulles, who yesterday (March 15, 1955) outlined a pattern of using new atomic devices for pinpoint military retaliation anywhere in the world. The twin statements by the President and Mr. Dulles were aimed at the Communists. Mr. Dulles indicated that it was up to Red China's leaders whether the tactical weapons would be used in the event of a Communist Chinese attack on Quemoy and Matsu Islands in the Pacific."

[65] *New York Times,* September, 1958.

[66] Testimony of Professor Allen S. Whiting, former chief of research and intelligence in the State Department, before

rumored that the use of atomic weapons in Indochina was again seriously debated at the time of the seige of the American garrison at Khe Sanh in 1968.[67] And as late as 1970 the Nixon administration deployed nuclear missiles in Taiwan capable of firing 600 miles into Chinese territory.[68]

Official threats or deliberate ambiguity concerning American willingness to resort to nuclear weapons are of course justified by the government as essential to the maintenance of a "credible deterrent." When such ambiguity is coupled with revelations of secret consideration of first use of nuclear weapons in numerous specific instances in Asia, then the situation cannot be dismissed as merely a game of bluff. It is indeed possible that the United States may choose to disregard world opinion and initiate nuclear war against China or in Southeast Asia. A number of secret contingency plans for the use of nuclear weapons in Southeast Asia are known to have been prepared for the government in the 1960s through such organizations as the Institute for Defense Analysis and RAND.[69] And in any future conflict with China, the pressures upon American policy makers

---

Senator Proxmire's Joint Economic Committee of Congress, August 11, 1971; cited in *I. F. Stone's Bi-Weekly*, September 6, 1971.

[67] See the articles by John W. Finney in the *New York Times*, February 15 and 16, 1968.

[68] Whiting, cited in *I. F. Stone's Bi-Weekly*, September 6, 1971.

[69] A good example of the "university-military complex": professors working in the "Jason" division of the IDA published a technical study of tactical nuclear weapons in 1964

for swift resort to the most destructive technology available would be immense. Former Secretary of State Dean Rusk emphasized this position as early as April 1964 in conversations with the premier of South Vietnam, Nguyen Khanh. According to censored portions of the *Pentagon Papers* made public by Jack Anderson, a cable from Saigon to Washington included this summary of the Rusk-Khanh talks:

The Secretary said he wished to emphasize [that] . . . if escalation brought about a major Chinese attack, it would also involve the use of nuclear arms. Many free world leaders would oppose this.

Chiang Kai-shek had told him fervently he did, and so did U Thant. Many Asians seemed to see an element of racial discrimination in use of nuclear arms; something we would do to Asians but not to Westerners.

Khanh replied he certainly had no quarrel with American use of nuclear arms, noted that decisive use of atomic bombs on Japan had in ending war saved not only American but also Japanese lives. One must use the force one had; if Chinese used masses of humanity, we would use superior fire power.

As late as July 1971 Rusk reiterated the view that most American decision makers "cannot imagine a war with China that would not be nuclear."[70]

---

and a report entitled "Tactical Nuclear Weapons in Southeast Asia" in 1967. See the brief report by Andrew Kopkind and James Ridgeway in Barnet, *Hard Times*, May 25–June 1, 1970.

[70] Anderson's column, "How We Play Kingmaker in Saigon," appeared in the October 12, 1971, issue of the *Madison Capitol-Times*; the cable does not appear to have been in-

The combination of cost-cutting and troop reductions which is fundamental to the Nixon Doctrine has long been emphasized by advocates of tactical nuclear weapons. In an article written a number of years ago by General Frederick H. Smith, Jr., both the economies of this option and the manner in which it might be applied in "insurgency" situations in Asia are described in some detail:

. . . a single nominal-yield nuclear weapon, airburst, will clear an area of forest about 8000 feet in radius. To achieve a similar effect with napalm would require 8000 sorties of F-100 aircraft, each carrying four 120-gallon drop tanks. Not only would 32,000 tanks have to be transported to the operating base but 25 million pounds of napalm would also have to be provided, over and above 8000 sorties worth of fuel. . . .

This country cannot afford the tremendous outlay in dollars, resources, and men needed to defeat aggression by man-to-man combat on the ground, supported only by high-explosive bombs and rockets, napalm, and machine-gun fire delivered from the air.

More specifically, General Smith advances a concept of "situation-control" targets—a theory which boils down to the nuclear destruction of those aspects of the terrain in Southeast Asia which presently aid guerrilla forces. In this scheme such targets or "situations" fall into eight categories: (1) rain forests

cluded subsequently in either the Senator Gravel or U.S. Government editions of the *Pentagon Papers*. Rusk's 1971 comment was quoted by Whiting and cited in *I. F. Stone's Bi-Weekly,* September 6, 1971.

(here nuclear bombs could create a "debris-belt barrier." If the enemy tried to cross it, they would provide "another lucrative nuclear target"); (2) valley routes through rain, deciduous, or bamboo forest ("Trees stripped of leaves and stem breakage would extend out to approximately 22,200 feet, leaving little or no cover to enemy forces"); (3) mangrove forests; (4) bamboo groves; (5) karst redoubt areas, that is, rough terrain characterized by eroded limestone formations in which caves and caverns afford protection to the enemy ("A bonus effect of surface burst . . . is residual radiation extending over approximately a one-mile diameter. Within this circle survival is possible only if exposure is limited to one hour and if personnel decontamination procedures were accomplished"); (6) mountain defiles, in which a nominal-yield nuclear weapon can block an enemy from his objective with deep craters or extensive landslides; (7) close contact seiges or redoubts (to protect the beseiged friendly troops from fallout, a cushion of at least 4,500 feet between them and the "perimeter of weapon effects" is advised, as is "air-ground coordination"); (8) beach or amphibious landings.[71]

A more recent sample of the relationship which some planners envision as existing between the Nixon Doctrine, technological advances, and nuclear weap-

[71] "Nuclear Weapons and Limited War," *Air University Quarterly Review*, Vol. XII, No. 1 (Spring 1960). This article is still regarded by insiders as one of the best available public summaries of the military evaluation of tactical nuclear weapons.

ons is to be found in an article by by Hanson Baldwin, former military editor of the *New York Times*.[72] "There must be no hesitancy in equipping" America's bases in the Western Pacific "with nuclear weapons for their own defense," Baldwin argued, and went on to note that:

the careful and precise use of an atomic shell, fired from an 8-inch howitzer, the utilization of atomic land mines to guard a fronteir (as now proposed by Turkey), the creation of a restricted and carefully controlled radioactive belt in virtually uninhabited country through which any aid from outside the country would have to pass, or the use of atomic demolition devices in thick jungle areas or in precipitous defiles to cause tangled "blow-downs" or landslides to block trails, roads or natural approach routes could substitute for manpower and add great power to the defense. . . .

In any case, tactical atomic weapons cannot be automatically foresworn if Asia is to be stabilized, for even their tacit invocation contributes to the "balance of terror" which—whether we like it or not—now governs the world we live in. And in any case, it is only by technological escalation, rather than by manpower escalation, that United States military forces can, without excessive cost in United States blood, redress within the immediate time frame of the near tomorrows the unfavorable manpower balance in Asia.

The "unfavorable manpower balance in Asia," which has long obsessed military thinkers such as Baldwin, is itself a telling commentary on the American im-

[72] "After Vietnam—What Military Strategy in the Far East?" *New York Times Magazine*, June 9, 1968.

perial consciousness. They lament and seek to re-dress, in brief, the fact that there are more Asians than Americans there.

The most tightly-reasoned argument that the Nixon Doctrine lowers the threshold of nuclear war in Asia has been advanced by a former director of the Asian Division, Systems Analysis, Office of the Secretary of Defense. Earl C. Ravenal, now associated with the Institute of Policy Studies, notes that while present U.S. military planning to a certain extent extends the conventional (nonnuclear) option in NATO, in Asia strategic thinking now has become strongly "biased toward the earlier use of nuclear weapons."[73] He cites a recent "quickened advocacy of nuclear re-liance in the public writings of middle grade military officers, journalist-strategists, and defense academies," as well as "strengthened institutional support for nu-clear alternative within the Office of the Secretary of Defense—notably among the International Security Affairs staff—that reinforces the persistent nuclear orientation of the Joint Chiefs of Staff and such sig-nificant unified commands as CINCPAC."[74] Through a close analysis of "the rigid logic of alternatives" im-plicit in the recent military-posture statements of President Nixon and Secretary Laird, Ravenal reaches this conclusion:

our amplified provision of a complementary role of sup-port, in a context of unrelieved forward defense of the territorial integrity of our client system, is still likely to

[73] Earl Ravenal, *Foreign Affairs* (January 1971), p. 209.
[74] Ravenal, "The Political-Military Gap," p. 37.

perpetuate conflict and to involve us in a contingency from the earliest moment, not simply at such later time as it began to appear that our military client could not "hack it." If the present Administration's program guarantees anything, it is that a future Asian crisis would be faced in an atmosphere of desperate improvisation. And should allied forces be threatened with collapse. U.S. decision-makers, facing the agonizing questions of deployment and mobilization, and considering respectfully the necessary reservations for NATO and other requirements, would be commensurately tempted to rise to nuclear threats, demon-strations, or strikes.[75]

The imperatives of the situation are sobering in-deed. Since 1945 the old objectives have twice led the United States into devastating wars in Asia. The immense cost of those wars plus the current Ameri-can economic crisis have fostered a new and precari-ous wedding of military strategy to cost-consciousness. The domestic political costs to an administration which commits American combat forces abroad are higher and more vividly apparent than they were in the 1950s and early 1960s. The new technologies of warfare remain far form perfected. Official rhapsodies to the contrary, "Asianization" can never attain even the level of performance achieved by American forces in Korea and Indochina. Poverty and repression in Asia, particularly under America's client regimes, make future insurgencies inevitable. And with the Laotian invasion, the United States has come very close to the limits of conventional escalation presently

[75] Ibid., p. 33.

available. Yet there has been no fundamental re-evaluation of American commitments and alliances abroad. The definition of "American interests in Asia" remains threateningly ambiguous. The conceit of America as an Asian power goes unchallenged (is China then an American power?). And meanwhile the nuclear weapons lie ready. The odds *may* be against the United States resorting to nuclear weapons in Asia. The odds, of course, were also presumably against American involvement in a land war in Asia after the Korean experience.

VII

The economic dimension of the Nixon Doctrine does not address root problems of underdevelopment and poses the danger of a new military-economic spiral in Asia. Economically as well as militarily, the low-profile role projected for the U.S. in Asia attempts to cloak extensive American pressure and involvement in a multinational guise. The new vocabulary of multinationalism, however, fails to obscure the fact that the development of the area will be dominated by the United States, its white allies, and Japan. In 1966, for example, Eugene R. Black, first president of the World Bank and a special adviser to President Johnson on Southeast Asian development, defended U.S. participation in the Asian Development Bank on the grounds that this would serve American national interests:

I think hat the nonregional (European) countries and Australi and New Zealand and Japan would have similar interests to ours, and I think that the vote at all times would certainly be favorable. As a matter of fact, in 15 years in the World Bank where I was, there practically never was any vote. There never was any question of the underdeveloped nations ganging up and voting.[76]

Although there are different views about what the underdeveloped countries of Asia offer more developed nations, the following attractions are obviously important: (1) raw materials (minerals, rubber, timber, and—especially in the light of recent discoveries—petroleum); (2) cheap labor for foreign-controlled light industries, including both manufacture of parts to be assembled in the home country and assembly plants for parts manufactured in the home country—neither process contributing much to the local economy (Japan, ironically, is particularly eager to exploit this human resource as its labor shortage increases and domestic wage levels rise); (3) a potential market for the products of the more industrialized countries (U.S. trade, as opposed to direct investment, is increasing faster in the Pacific than in Europe); and (4) the opportunity for an early and potentially lucrative role in the basic economic and financial institutions of the area (to take Indonesia as an example, since the 1966 coup fifteen American banks have opened offices in the country and it is estimated that two-thirds of the planned investments

[76] U. S. Senate Committee on Foreign Relations, Hearings, *Asian Development Bank Act*, 89th Congress, 2d Session, February 16, 1966; quoted in Peter Wiley, "Vietnam and the Pacific Rim Strategy," *Leviathan* (June 1969).

will be American owned).[77] There are also lesser attractions: the neocolonialist life style of the overseas businessman, for example, and the possibility frequently mentioned by Japanese industrialists of curbing environmental pollution in Japan by relocating plants which cause pollution in third world countries.

When one questions whether the advanced capitalist countries offer a real hope to the *peoples* of Southeast Asia, however, the answers are less easily forthcoming. Past examples and present trends, in Latin America as well as Asia itself, suggest that reliance upon "multinational" aid, trade, and investment along the lines Mr. Nixon seems to have in mind will create or consolidate native elites more intent upon personal aggrandizement than on public works; will exacerbate rather than resolve existing schisms between city and countryside and between rich and poor; will foster a system of "industrial dualism" in which a favored sector of manufactures is encouraged and protected to the neglect of a far larger sector of native crafts and cottage industries; and will lock the recipient countries into a permanently inferior and dependent relationship with the advanced capitalistic countries. These distortions— and the corruption and glut of services and luxury consumer items for the native elite which invariably accompanies them—are already apparent in the Philippines, Thailand, South Vietnam, South Korea, and elsewhere in "free" Asia. Thus two economists ob-

[77] Wiley, "Vietnam and the Pacific Rim Strategy," p. 7.

serve that "in human terms, the result of the last twenty-five years has meant abysmally low levels of consumption, education, health and welfare for about two-thirds of the people" of Southeast Asia.[78] A United Nations report of 1965 describes the situation as presenting "a scene of contrast, with some indications of considerable progress standing out against a background of extensive poverty, hunger, illiteracy, and sickness."[79] And Gunnar Myrdal notes that "the extent of inequality has either remained constant over the past decade (or longer) or has increased."[80]

By assigning the countries of Southeast Asia a specific role in the international capitalist system as suppliers of raw materials and recipients of advanced manufactured goods, danger exists that these economies will be skewed in such a way as to relegate them to a state of permanent underdevelopment. Since the world market price of raw materials has been generally declining, while the price of consumer and capital goods is rising, the underdeveloped nations drawn into the capitalist system in this manner face the prospects of a chronic trade imbalance; a

[78] Peter F. Bell and Stephen A. Resnick, "The Contradictions of Postwar Development in Southeast Asia," *The Journal of Contemporary Asia*, Vol. I, No 1 (London, June 1970).

[79] United Nations, *Economic Bulletin for Asia and Far East*, Vol. XVI, No 1 (June 1965), p. 16; cited in Bell and Resnick, "The Contradictions of Postwar Development in Southeast Asia."

[80] Gunnar Myrdal, *Asian Drama: An Inquiry into the Poverty of Nations* (New York: Pantheon, 1968), pp. 565–566; cited in Bell and Resnick, "The Contradictions of Postwar Development in Southeast Asia."

drain on foreign exchange reserves, and a permanent inability to develop their own light or heavy industries in the face of Western and Japanese competition, pressure, and priorities. Nor do past trends in foreign investment and aid offer real hope that future "multinational" efforts will provide underdeveloped countries the capital necessary to establish a balanced base for future economic development. Between 1950 and 1965, for example, direct U.S. investment in underdeveloped countries totaled $9 billion, while the return to the U.S. from these countries was $25.6 billion, for a net outflow of $16.6 billion or about a billion dollars a year—certainly far more than the internal wealth stimulated by the initial investments.[81] Similarly, most U.S. foreign aid has been structured so that in one way or another it benefits the U.S. in the end (whether given as interest-bearing loans, or tied to purchases of U.S. goods or transportation in U.S. carriers, or directed to projects which will benefit U.S. investors in the long run).

Japan, which will join the U.S. as the major force in future Asian development projects under the Nixon Doctrine, is proving even more adept at the same game. Already established in East and Southeast Asia as a major importer of raw materials and exporter of finished products ranging from packaged noodles to complete industrial plants, the Japanese thrust is viewed with strong but mixed feelings

[81] Committee of Concerned Asian Scholars, ed., *The Indochina Story* (New York: Bantam, 1970; Pantheon, 1971), ch. 31.

throughout Asia. While the Nixon Doctrine postulates Japan as a keystone to economic "regionalism" in Asia, many Asian leaders, on the contrary, view Japan as a potential threat to regional stability. Thus Adam Malik, Indonesia's foreign minister, has stated bluntly that "The main threat to Southeast Asia is from Japan."[82] The mayor of Manila recently lambasted the "insidious Nipponization of the Philippines."[83] A Malaysian official complains, "We didn't gain political independence from the British just to become the economic serfs of the Japanese."[84] And current articles on Japan's economic expansion into Asia commonly include quotations such as this by the chairman of the Philippine Senate Economic Affairs Committee: "We realize that the Japanese are getting through commerce what they failed to achieve through the war."[85]

Such fear has roots in Asian memories of the brutal exploitation of Japan's earlier "Co-Prosperity Sphere," less than three decades ago. But a more immediate, hard fact lies behind Asia's distrust of Japan: up to now Japan appears to be taking far more out of its neighbors than it is putting into them. To borrow a phrase from the *Wall Street Journal*, Japan's trade with Asia (as with the U.S.) is "lopsided traffic."

[82] *Interplay: the Magazine of International Affairs*, Vol. III, No. 15 (December 1970), p. 20. Jon Sherwood has called my attention to several of the articles cited here concerning Japan's economic expansion.

[83] *Time*, May 10, 1971, p. 84.

[84] *Wall Street Journal*, May 12, 1971.

[85] *Fortune*, September 1970, p. 127; cf. *Wall Street Journal*, May 12, 1971.

Japanese exports to the Asia-Pacific area in 1970 totaled approximately $5.3 billion, while purchases were estimated at $3 billion (iron ore, copper, tin, lumber, rubber, food, "some driblets of oil").[86] South Korea's trade with Japan shows an unfavorable balance of roughly six to one. Taiwan is also in the red, as are Thailand, Hong Kong, and Singapore. And the trend appears to be accelerating. U.S. Assistant Secretary of State for Economic Affairs Philip H. Trezise has predicted that Japanese exports will more than double to nearly $42 billion by 1975, with an astonishing trade surplus of $12 billion. And he warns: "I seriously question whether the international system can stand a Japanese global trade balance of $12 billion in 1975."[87]

The sanguine point of view holds that the combination of Japanese investment and aid, along with trade, will stimulate the underdeveloped economies of Asia, and scattered sectors *have* benefited from the Japanese economic invasion. Even Japanese "aid," however, is proving a dubious blessing. Japan's leaders now regularly reaffirm their intention of increasing foreign aid to Asia to 1 percent of GNP; the Nixon Doctrine makes much of this, and indeed the U.S. has long been pressuring Japan to raise its niggardly contributions in this area. As Tunku Abdul Rahman, former Prime Minister of Malaysia, noted in Japan in August 1970, however, Japanese aid has

[86] *Wall Street Journal,* May 5, 1970; cf. *Time,* October 4, 1971.

[87] *Fortune,* September 1970, p. 127.

been structured to give with one hand while taking away twice as much with the other. The *Asahi shimbun* agreed with the Tunku that Japan's aid program was a "pump-primer for export promotion."[88] Under the rubric of "economic cooperation," nearly half of Japan's aid to developing countries has been in the form of export credits for the purchase of Japanese products. Japanese interest rates are also high: "ranging from 8.25 percent in the case of commercial bank credits, to 5 and 6 percent for credits given by the government-backed export-import bank. And aid terms to desperate mendicants like Indonesia have by no means been generous in terms of either time or cost."[89] The $500 million in aid which Japan provided South Korea following normalization of relations in 1965, for example, was used to spring the Korean market wide open to Japan.[90]

Japanese investment in Asia, high in South Korea and Taiwan but overall still at a preliminary level, is similarly a two-edged sword. Primarily geared to opening markets capable of absorbing the cascade of Japanese exports, the experience of Taiwan, South Korea, and Thailand has been that, given the enter-

[88] *Far Eastern Economic Review,* December 12, 1970, p. 45. For an excellent general critique of Japan's developing economic impact on Asia see Jim Shoch, "Japan: Rising Sun in Asia," *Pacific Research & World Empire Telegram,* Vol. I, No. 2 (September 1969).

[89] Varindra Tarzie Vittachi, "Asian Views on Japan: Model or Monster?" *Interplay* (December 1970), p. 23; cf. Louis Kraar, "How the Japanese Mount That Export Blitz," *Fortune,* September 1970, p. 172.

[90] *The Economist,* November 21, 1970.

ing wedge, Japanese investors are able and willing to take over. Taiwan, for example, has already found it necessary to exclude Japanese from further investment in several sectors of its economy in order to preserve a measure of local control.[91] In South Korea, local control seems already past recall. Japan controls 90.2 percent of South Korea's chemical fertilizer industry, 64.1 percent of its chemical fiber industry, 43.5 percent of its industrial chemical industry, 62 percent of its foodstuffs industry, and 48.3 percent of its cement and glassmaking industry. Insofar as joint Japanese-South Korean ventures are concerned ("multinationalism" in acion), it was calculated in 1970 that Japanese firms controlled less than half the stock in 19 percent of such ventures, half the stock in 33 percent, over half in 22 percent, and 100 per cent in 26 percent of all joint ventures. In other words, more than 80 percent of Japanese businesses with direct capital investments in South Korea own over half the stock in their Korean branches and control the management. The wages of industrial workers in South Korea and Taiwan are one-fourth to one-fifth the level in Japan, and both countries have imposed severe restrictions on labor to facilitate the capital development permitted by this imbalance.[92] For the underdeveloped countries of Asia, the "economic regionalism" promised by the Nixon

[91] *Wall Street Journal*, May 5, 1971.
[92] Statistics on South Korea are from Herbert Bix, whose study of the economic relationship between Japan and Korea will appear in a forthcoming volume on Korea published by Pantheon, edited by Frank Baldwin.

Doctrine may in fact prove to be little more than a bitter choice between remaining neocolonies of the West or becoming part of Japan's long dreamed of "Co-Prosperity Sphere."

The problem of development is further compounded by the peculiar relationship between American military spending and the growth of Asian capitalism since 1945. The postwar economic growth of South Korea, South Vietnam, Taiwan, Thailand, Singapore, Japan, and the Philippines has been greatly accelerated by American expenditures for the wars in Korea and Vietnam, by maintenance of the huge American network of bases in Asia; and by growth in domestic U.S. market sparked by American defense spending. In 1970, for example, it was estimated that Japanese industry was doing about $1 billion worth of business a year directly or indirectly related to the war in Indochina.[93] In Thailand the U.S. has invested $500 million just in the construction of six major air bases for the bombing of Laos and Vietnam, with extensive additional funds going into the construction of the deepwater port of Sattahip on the Gulf of Siam. Half of the increase in the gross domestic product of Thailand between 1965 and 1967 derived from U.S. military spending within the country. In 1970 the *New York Times* noted that "The closing of the air bases, and the withdrawal of the airmen stationed on them, would have a shattering impact on the Thai economy, just as

[93] *The Providence Sunday Journal,* February 8, 1970.

their construction and the presence of the men has worked profound changes in the economic and cultural patterns in rural Thailand."[94] As mentioned above, in South Korea dollar earnings directly connected with the Vietnam war totaled almost $400 million in 1968 and 1969 alone; this was in addition to $403 million in U.S. military assistance funds in fiscal 1968, $140 million in fiscal 1969, and in the neighborhood of $200 million in fiscal 1970. According to a recent report prepared under Professor Franz Schurmann at the University of California at Berkeley:

the Korean economy finds itself in a rather precarious position. While her trade deficit has thus far been covered by loans from the U.S. and Japan, these loans must now be paid back. By 1972 repayments will reach over $200 million. This in turn promises to strip her of much needed future growth capital. As long as Korea is involved in Vietnam she can earn enough foreign exchange to meet these commitments but with the eventual conclusion of the war she must either default, renegotiate, or find new sources of capital.[95]

The road to Asian capitalism has been paved by the American military, and it remains a serious but generally neglected question as to whether the growth rate of America's "free world" allies in Asia has not become to a greater or lesser extent dependent upon

[94] *New York Times,* January 3, 1970; Bell and Resnick, "The Contradictions of Postwar Development in Southeast Asia."

[95] *America in Asia,* p. 12.

such war-related stimulants. The predominantly military focus of the Nixon Doctrine, with its stress on military assistance and strengthening of the military capacities of the various pro-American regimes in Asia, is not inconsistent with this trend. To Asians, whatever their political persuasion, capitalism and militarism are openly and inseparably linked.

These considerations lock into the more purely military dimension of the Nixon Doctrine. If the economic development of the countries of Southeast Asia proceeds in such a way as to exacerbate the hardships of the majority, insurgency can be expected to increase, with an increasingly high content of revolutionary nationalism directed against the foreign presence. The primary focus of U.S. aid to its client governments is already military to begin with. This will increase even more, particularly as the stakes of the "multinational" corporations and organizations in preserving the political, social, and economic *status quo* in the various countries increase. And one can anticipate that such a rise in tensions would also be accompanied by a rise in the number of advocates of solutions by resort to technological, even nuclear, escalation.

The discovery of potentially vast oil resources along the shores of Southeast Asia has already introduced this issue into the Indochina War. Washington and Saigon are keenly aware of the feeble economic base of the South Vietnamese government, and the success or failure of "economic Vietnamization" will help determine the fate of both Mr. Nixon's

Doctrine and his client regimes. Ambassador Bunker addressed this problem in a speech to the American Chamber of Commerce in Saigon on February 15, 1971:

Therefore, an effective strategy must be designed to further participation in foreign trade and to attract private investment from abroad. All of you here today can help to forge and further this strategy. I think you may also serve your own economic best interest, as well as America's and Viet-Nam's, by convincing other American companies of the merits of doing business here. The recent petroleum law and the new investment law now before the upper House indicate the Government's desire to create a flexible long-term investment policy which will serve Viet-Nam's interests while at the same time it creates an economic climate foreign investors will find attractive. . . . Everything I have been discussing until now may be put under the heading of Vietnamization.[96]

Nine days later the National Liberation Front denounced the Saigon oil law and declared that oil concessions granted to foreign concerns by the Thieu regime would be regarded as null and nonbinding by the NLF.[97] Although the international oil companies are playing their cards close to the chest, it is known that intense competition (and bribery) is taking place for the South Vietnamese offshore leases, with American and Japanese interests in the center of the

[96] *Department of State Bulletin,* February 15, 1971, pp. 209–210. This and the next several quotations are included in a useful digest of the oil issue prepared by the American Friends Service Committee, 160 North 15th Street, Philadelphia, Pennsylvania 19102.

[97] *Le Monde,* February 27, 1971.

scramble. The dilemma this bodes is essentially this: (1) to encourage investment by foreign oil firms at the present time, it seems inevitable that the Nixon administration will have to guarantee survival of an anticommunist regime in Saigon; (2) once entrenched, the oil companies can be expected to provide powerful support to the Saigon regime in its pursuit of a military solution rather than negotiated peace in Vietnam. According to an oil industry publication in March 1971, the Defense Department has offered "to help foot investment insurance to U.S. companies for any future offshore South Vietnam oil exploration and development."[98] The haste in which Saigon, Washington, and the American and Japanese oil firms have been pushing this issue thus strongly suggests that true "self-determination" for the peoples of Southeast Asia is not on the agenda of the Nixon Doctrine.

VIII

In the international realm, severe and potentially explosive contradictions belie the new presidential rhetoric of "multilateralism." In his February 25, 1971, address, Mr. Nixon paid considerable homage to "a new era of multilaterial diplomacy," "the creative possibilities of a pluralistic world," "a new international structure in the Pacific area." His new doctrine for Asia allegedly aims at a dynamic synthesis of Asian regionalism and great-power diplo-

[98] *Platt's Oilgram News Service,* March 10, 1971

macy—a new structure which will "rest on two pillars: the collective interests of Asian nations acting in regional groupings, and the policies of the four major powers concerned with the region." The four great powers, of course, are the U.S., China, Japan, and the Soviet Union. No one denies the extraordinary tensions which exist both among the four powers and between these powers and the weaker nations of Asia. In many respects, however, the Nixon Doctrine, including the administration's handling of the new policy toward China, has exacerbated rather than diminished these tensions. The situation of Japan can be taken as an example.

It has long been a cliché among students of America's Far Eastern policy that in the course of the last century the United States has rarely been able to manage friendly relations with both China and Japan simultaneously. Like balloons joined at the stem, the good image of one is inflated only at the expense of the other, and policy and concrete actions (and disasters) follow accordingly. However valid this cliché may be, it is obvious that the present high point of postwar Sino-American goodwill has been accompanied by the postwar nadir in the U.S.-Japan relationship. Japan, touted by the President as a key to the Nixon Doctrine, has also been treated by the President and his spokesmen as the potential scourge of the "new structure" in Asia. As China's image in the U.S. is revised in a more positive direction, Japan is increasingly described in terms of irresponsibility and potential military recklessness.

A similar change has occurred in China's foreign policy pronouncements in the last year or so, with Japan replacing the United States as the avowed primary threat to stability. This complex situation is ironic, dangerous, and very possibly enduring.

Many of the current sources of U.S.-Japan friction are common knowledge. The paradoxes are perhaps less obvious. On the open level these issues between the two leading capitalist powers stand out: America's $2.7 billion trade deficit with Japan (most dramatically in textiles, electronics, and automobiles); restrictions on imports and foreign capital investment in Japan; competition in world markets; American resentment over niggardly Japanese aid to the third world as well as the "free ride" in defense; Japanese resentments over Okinawa, American bases in Japan, the recent U.S. protective tariff, and American pressures to devalue the yen; and a burgeoning nationalistic resentment over the extent to which Japan has been pressured into conformity with American foreign policy since 1945. The cavalier manner in which President Nixon treated the Japanese in announcing both his new China policy (three minutes advance notice) and his new economic policy (ten minutes advance notice) hardly impressed them as an effective example of dialogue in action. But the problems run deeper.

On one level the dilemma is military, and since the Japan-Okinawa military complex is the very heart of the American forward posture in Asia, developments in this area are central to understanding the implications of the Nixon Doctrine. The horns of the dilemma are these: the administration proposes the reduction of the American military establishment in Japan and Okinawa and Japanese assumption of many of the functions hitherto assigned to American forces in Asia. But at the same time, there is emerging in the United States and elsewhere increasing fear that Japan is on the verge of remilitarizing on a massive scale, including development of nuclear weapons and creation of a large navy, and that American withdrawal will accelerate such trends. Like a giant who has rolled a huge boulder to the peak of a mountain and now fears it will roll down out of control, the United States finds itself in a quandry.

The irony of this situation is nowhere clearer than in the writings of Edwin Reischauer, former ambassador to Japan (1961–1966) and the best-known publicist for the U.S.-Japan alliance. Up to the early 1960s, Professor Reischauer devoted himself both publicly and privately to encouraging Japanese rearmament with the ostensible goal of permitting the gradual phasing out of the direct American role in Japan and Okinawa. During his tour as ambassador, however, his emphasis began to shift to stressing the importance of the military alliance as a means of curbing Japanese remilitarization. Recently Professor Reischauer has become one of the most effective conjurers of the vision of an unleashed, militaristic Japan. In March 1970, for example, he acknowledged Japan's rapid military expansion and noted that for many years his force has been more than adequate "to quell domestic 'disturbances.'" It was his impression then that there was "in Washington . . . a great deal more fear that Japan will over-arm than desire for her to expand her military power," and he went on to note that "in my recent trips to Japan I have sensed a rising urge among Japanese to be a great military, perhaps even nuclear, power. They have a nagging fear that a nation cannot be a 'great country' (*taikoku*) merely through economic strength or cultural influence but must also be a nuclear power."[99] With the events of the summer of 1971, the gesture toward Peking and the heightened U.S.-Japan tensions, Professor Reischauer voiced his plea for going slow in any modification of the U.S.-Japan military *status quo* even more strongly:

Without bases in Japan and the tacit support of the Japanese, the United States would almost inevitably be forced to withdraw its military power from the whole area. In that case the Japanese—dependent as they are for their livelihood on a vast seaborne commerce, deeply feared and resented by the Chinese and their other neighbors, and surrounded by the military instability in Korea and Southeast Asia—would unquestionably feel insecure with only their present minuscule naval power. The building of a sizable fleet would seem to them only common sense. To the Chinese and other East Asians, however, such a step would appear to verify their worst fears.

[99] *Christianity and Crisis*, March 2, 1970. Professor Reischauer's comments came in response to an article by Jerry K. Fisher in the January 19, 1970, issue of the same magazine.

Tensions would mount, and hostile reactions from Japan's neighbors would spur further Japanese defense efforts. The Japanese might drift into becoming a major military power and, ultimately, a member of the nuclear club. If a trend in this direction starts, then more relaxed Sino-American relations would have been more than offset by increased Sino-Japanese strains, and even Japanese-American relations might drift back toward the suspicion and hostility that characterized them in the past—indeed a disastrous tradeoff.[100]

But has there not been a ruthless logic inherent in the entire course of postwar American relations with Japan which has brought the situation to this impasse? And can there be a meaningful new policy for Asia if the military alternatives in this pivot area, Japan and Ckinawa, are limited to continued high American presence, or a slow creation of Japanese-American military tradeoffs at the same high level, or massive Japanese remilitarization?

Articulation of the Japan dilemma is new only to American spokesmen. China and the other countries of Asia have been voicing similar fears since the late 1940s, but these were consistently dismissed by American officials and "Japan specialists" as mcre propaganda. It was scarcely noted at the time that the critics of Japan spoke in terms of that country's dangerous *potential* once the way to remilitarization was opened. Thoughtful critics in the early postwar period asked the United States to think a generation ahead—that is, to the 1970s—and went a step further

[100] *New York Times Magazine*, September 19, 1971.

to relate the problem of Japanese remilitarization to the nature of the developing Japanese and American economic empires. China's present denunciations of Japan are consistent with this long-term analysis, and it is significant that with the possible exception of the Sino-Soviet dispute, virtually all of the issues which China now singles out as major threats to stability in Asia involve Japan. These include Indochina (where Japan profits from the war and is increasingly frank about securing its strategic interests in that area to protect its global "lifeline"); Korea (where Japan's support of the South Korean regime and immense economic involvement threaten to draw Japan immediately into any flare-up of the Korean civil conflict); Taiwan (where the burgeoning Japanese economic role since 1965 undergirds Japan's support for a "two-China" policy); and Japan itself (where growing ultranationalism plus concrete proposals such as the Fourth Defense Plan point directly to militarism, while on a more indirect and theoretical level, the "lop-sided" nature of her economic development is believed to make Japan's military expansion abroad inevitable.[101]

One of the great tragedies of contemporary Asia, as Japan's Prime Minister Eisaku Sato recently noted, is the existence of the divided countries: China,

[101] The Fourth Defense Plan, issued in conjunction with a Defense White Paper in October 1970, calls for a military budget of approximately $16 billion over a five year period beginning in 1972, a sum over 2.2 times that spent under the Third Defense Plan. The Japanese threat as seen from China was strongly expressed by Chou En-lai in his interviews with both James Reston and the delegation representing the Com-

Korea, Vietnam. These divisions have caused wars in the past; they remain the tinder boxes for future wars. It is becoming increasingly clear to Western scholars working on the postwar period that the United States bears an extraordinarily heavy responsibility for the initial creation of these divisions. And it has also become apparent that during Mr. Sato's own term as premier, Japan has begun to assume a major role in the freezing of these divisions and heightening of these tensions. As the U.S. falters in its course of "free world" empire in Asia, Japan has moved in economically to help shore up the regimes in South Korea, Taiwan, and South Vietnam. The supporters of the Nixon Doctrine urge, and the doctrine's critics fear, that this will soon be followed by Japanese military commitments concerning these areas.

Like the military dilemma in the U.S.-Japan relationship, the economic issue is double-edged for the United States. For two decades American policy makers have abetted Japan's entry into world markets as part of their global cold war economic policy. The assumption was, as the U.S. ambassador to Japan phrased it in 1954, that there was "room for all of us" in the markets of the Far East—all, that is, of the industrialized countries of the free world.[102] Com-

---

mittee of Concerned Asian Scholars in the summer of 1971; this issue has been developed in great detail in the Chinese press over the course of the last few years—and indeed since the late 1940s.

[102] Robert Murphy in *Department of State Bulletin,* March 22, 1954, p. 531.

petition could be expected, it was argued, but this was the essence of capitalism and would work to the benefit of all concerned. That policy line, however, has been challenged at almost precisely the same time that Japan is actually beginning to reap the fruits of the great "free market" in Asia. Again an ironic contradiction: The Nixon Doctrine calls for an expanding Japanese economic role in Asia. But the Nixon anti-Japanese tariff, and the recent alarmist pronouncements of America's industrialists, indicate doubts that there is still room for all of us everywhere any longer. More and more one notes the vocabulary of the 1930s appearing in the polemics of the 1970s—in talk of Japan's increasingly wide-flung "lifelines," and ominous presentiments of global trade wars.

These aspects of the Japan dilemma are but a suggestion of the complex of relations among the four great powers. The Sino-Soviet dispute has been looked upon as an opportunity by U.S. policy makers, but the game of exploiting tensions between the two countries is a dangerous one and any effort to improve relations with one threatens to worsen relations with the other. Despite China's denunciations of Japan and Japan's ties to Taiwan, powerful forces within both countries are working to bring about *rapprochement* between them.[103] Japan's relations with China are further complicated, however, by her

[103] The complexity of these more hopeful trends in Sino-Japanese relations can be seen in the stand on China recently taken by Yasuhiro Nakasone, one of the most powerful mem-

growing economic interests in the development of the eastern USSR. At the same time the Soviet-Japanese relationship is complicated by unresolved territorial disputes between the two countries (as well as a deep historic distrust which traces back to the nineteenth century). And while the U.S.-Japan relationship is showing great strains, it remains true that broad common interests still join the two countries. It may indeed be possible to turn these very contradictions into the beginning of a "creative pluralism" in Asia. History, the temper of the present administration, and the concrete problems already discussed in this essay, however, suggest that this is unlikely.

Tensions among the great powers are so complex that policy makers and critics alike tend to address these issues at the expense of the weaker nations— and at the expense of the peoples of Asia themselves. It is axiomatic in traditional power politics that

bers of the ruling Liberal-Democratic party in Japan. As head of the Defense Agency in 1970, Nakasone bore primary responsibility for the Fourth Defense Plan and the Defense White Paper which are widely regarded as blueprints for Japan's rapid militarization. But in September 1971, Nakasone broke ranks with the official policy of his party and defended the position that Peking is the sole legitimate government of China, and Taiwan is an integral part of China (*New York Times,* September 13, 1971). A similar position was taken earlier by the former Japanese Foreign Minister Aiichiro Fujiyama, who also accused the Foreign Ministry of "just following the Washington line" on the two-China policy, and, like Professor Reischauer, expressed fear that "the younger generation" in Japan "is increasingly showing interest in war, if not accepting it." *Far Eastern Economic Review,* February 13, 1971, p. 33.

smaller countries become pawns. And as the *Pentagon Papers* revealed, when a great power such as the United States shapes its policy with a myopic fixation upon American "interests" and power "realities," the people of those weaker nations become expendable. This is one of the simplest and yet most profound lessons which the United States could learn from its interventions in the Chinese revolution, the Korean civil war, and the anticolonial struggle in Indochina—and in the internal affairs of client states throughout Asia. The peoples of much of Asia have paid the price of death and destruction. Rather than being provided a "breathing space," they have been held back and perhaps completely prevented from shaping their own destinies. The United States and the world have gained neither peace nor freedom nor stability nor well-being, but rather the terrible distortions of American and international society today. Yet the lessons drawn by American policy makers remain technocratic ones, and power issues rather than human issues continue to guide policy.[104]

For the people of the weaker nations of Asia, the Nixon Doctrine offers little indeed. Within those countries it continues to support the same type of generally corrupt, repressive, exploitative—but pro-American—regimes which the United States has sup-

[104] Thus for the President, the "lessons to be learned from our Vietnam experience" are "about unconventional warfare and the role of outside countries, the nature of commitments, the balance of responsibilities, the need for public understanding and support" (from the second State of the World message). The critique of power politics naturally does not apply to the United States alone.

ported in the past. The "regional groupings" taken seriously by the administration still tend to coincide with the so-called free world camp, and it is difficult to perceive in this area any departure from the past policy of enforced bipolarization. American support invariably goes to those elements in a country who in external affairs support the United States and in internal affairs endorse private enterprise and are tolerant of considerable foreign investment. The result is to exacerbate polarization within the society on the one hand, and on the other hand to make adherence to an independent role in diplomacy extremely difficult for weaker nations caught in the web of the American empire. There is, in fact, a greater degree of national sovereignty and independence in foreign affairs within the "communist camp" in Asia than among the nations of "free Asia."[105] The latter remain heavily reliant upon American aid, greatly indebted to America's postwar military spending and wars in Asia for much of their economic growth; increasingly dependent upon a market system dominated by the United States and Japan; and predominantly judged not by their contribution to the well-being of their people, but rather by their anticommunist credentials and contributions, real or potential, to American "interests" in Asia.

Implicit in much of the preceding discussion is the belief that the poverty and misery under which many of Asia's millions toil derives as much from a social

[105] Cf. chapter 25 in Committee of Concerned Scholars, ed., *The Indochina Story.*

and political malaise as from an economic dilemma; that the military issue is branch and not root.[106] Many policy makers and academics would agree with this, yet few are willing to face seriously the dilemma which has been consistently posed by American reliance upon "anticommunist reformist elites." In the Nixon Doctrine also, the focus remains on attempting to bring about change through military or urban elites which, as case after case has shown, can rarely carry out thorough-going and meaningful reforms without undermining their own privileged position In Indochina, this is readily apparent in the venal puppet regimes in Saigon, Phnompenh, and Vientiane. Outside the war theater it is equally obvious, although less publicized. Consider, for example, the Philippines, where seven decades of intimate American involvement culminated in the "democracy" of the 1969 elections.

Filipinos view elections as a confirmation of the power of the wealthy business and landed interests who back both parties but usually pick the winners before Election Day and quietly give them the most support. In this case they picked President Marcos.

For the Philippine peasantry, three-fourths of the population, living standards have not risen since the

[106] A recent example can be seen in the abuse of one of the technological innovations in which humane men saw great hope for the third world—the "green revolution" of miracle seeds which was to eliminate starvation forever. See Thomas B. Wiens, "Seeds of Revolution," *Bulletin of Concerned Asian Scholars*, Vol. II, No. 3 (April–July 1970). Also *Far Eastern Economic Review*, September 21, 1969, p. 773.

Spanish occupation.[107]

The Nixon Doctrine glosses over this side of the Asian dilemma. Also ignored or disparaged is the other and more hopeful side of the dilemma, namely, the dynamic of social and political change which has thus far proven itself most viable in underdeveloped, largely peasant societies: revolutionary change initiated in the countryside, calling upon the energies of the people themselves, and motivated not by an attempt to siphon off discontent which might feed "insurgency" or threaten "stability," but rather by a fundamental desire to alleviate misery.

The administration claims to recognize a new era in Asia. At best, however, this recognition can only be described as a grudging endeavor to reconcile new power realities with other changing political, economic, and military considerations with the least possible sacrifice of old shibboleths concerning the nature and needs of Asia's peoples and America's proper role toward them. The Nixon Doctrine is good domestic politics, perhaps; it is obviously high time for the low posture at home. It has its elements of high drama. But it is hardly statesmanship, and indeed little more than one would have expected to be tossed up in any case by the normal course of time, technology, bureaucracy, economic imperatives, and imperial pride. And that is far from enough.

[107] *New York Times*, November 16, 1969. Philippine U. N. Ambassador Salvador Lopez, "The Colonial Relationship," in *The United States and the Philippines*, F. H. Golay, ed. (Engelwood Cliffs, N. J.: Prentice-Hall, 1966).

72 73 74   12 11 10 9 8 7 6 5 4 3 2